ADJUNCT FACULTY VOICES

new FACULTY MAJORITY

Current and forthcoming titles publishing in our
NEW FACULTY MAJORITY
series

CONTINGENT ACADEMIC LABOR
Evaluating Conditions to Improve
Student Outcomes
Daniel B. Davis
Foreword by Adrianna Kezar

**SUPPORTING THE NEW FACULTY
MAJORITY**
Embracing Collegiality on Campus
Don Haviland, Nathan F. Alleman, and
Cara Allen Cliburn Allen

Available Winter 2018

ADJUNCT FACULTY VOICES

Cultivating Professional Development and Community at the Front Lines of Higher Education

Edited by

Roy Fuller, Marie Kendall Brown,

and Kimberly Smith

Series Foreword by Maria Maisto
Foreword by Adrianna Kezar

The New Faculty Majority series

STERLING, VIRGINIA

Published by Stylus Publishing, LLC.
22883 Quicksilver Drive
Sterling, Virginia 20166-2102

Library of Congress Cataloging-in-Publication Data

Names: Fuller, Roy, editor. | Brown, Marie Kendall, editor. |
Smith, Kimberly, 1991- editor.
Title: Adjunct faculty voices : cultivating professional development and community at the front lines of higher education/
dited by Roy Fuller, Marie Kendall Brown, and Kimberly Smith.
Description: First edition. |
Sterling, Virginia : Stylus Publishing, 2017. |
Includes bibliographical references and index.
Identifiers: LCCN 2017009838 (print) |
LCCN 2017032586 (ebook) |
ISBN 9781620363737 (uPDF) |
ISBN 9781620363744 (ePUB, mobi) |
ISBN 9781620363713 (cloth : alk. paper) |
ISBN 9781620363720 (pbk. : alk. paper) |
ISBN 9781620363737 (library networkable e-edition) |
ISBN 9781620363744 (consumer e-edition)
Subjects: LCSH: College teachers, Part-time--Professional
relationships--United States. | College teachers, Part-time--
Vocational guidance--United States. |
Universities and colleges--United States--Faculty. |
College personnel management--United States.
Classification: LCC LB2331.72 (ebook) |
LCC LB2331.72 .A34 2017 (print) |
DDC 378.1/2--dc23
LC record available at https://lccn.loc.gov/2017009838

13-digit ISBN: 978-1-62036-371-3 (cloth)
13-digit ISBN: 978-1-62036-372-0 (paperback)
13-digit ISBN: 978-1-62036-373-7 (library networkable e-edition)
13-digit ISBN: 978-1-62036-374-4 (consumer e-edition)

Printed in the United States of America

All first editions printed on acid-free paper
that meets the American National Standards Institute
Z39-48 Standard.

First Edition, 2017

We dedicate this work to adjunct faculty whose voices are too often not heard and whose love of teaching and students calls them to continue their good work.

CONTENTS

TABLES

FOREWORD

This book highlights an important concept to understanding the changes occurring with the faculty—contingency has destroyed community that existed to support professional standards, expectations, and support. Without such a community, a quality teaching and learning environment is difficult to achieve and teaching effectiveness hampered. This book highlights how the isolation of adjunct faculty contributes not only to their job satisfaction but also to their ability to advance as professionals and to partake in a professional community. In fact, one of the underlying components of being a professional is sharing norms and standards with a collective group around a particular work practice. The very notion of being a professional is challenged, if not undone, by contingent faculty roles.

The authors not only address a highly important concept but also take a novel approach by highlighting the stories of adjunct faculty and bringing them together with faculty developers who have found, been offered, or taken advantage of professional development opportunities. They join the voices of adjunct faculty with the administrators on campus who have made it their responsibility to provide greater support and, over time, a community for these faculty.

The stories of adjunct faculty are the foundation and core of this work. And the authors firmly believe in the power of stories to create, galvanize, and motivate change.

> Stories that evocatively capture the lived experiences of contingent faculty can add to the flame that has been lit in a dark corner of academia. If students are to succeed in a globally competitive environment that demands skill sets of critical thinking, intercultural competence, and writing and communication skills (among myriad specialized skills), how can institutions continue to treat

the majority of the faculty body as second-class academics, at-will employees, and exploited educators? (p. 44, this volume).

The stories shared range from adjunct faculty who have attended professional development conferences and describe their experience trying to invite others to undergo a similar process; adjunct faculty who develop a community of practice, experimenting in the classroom, availing themselves of professional development; to seeking out mentors and the like. But these everyday activities take on greater complexity when engaged by adjunct faculty who juggle intense workloads, work at multiple institutions, and are isolated from their colleagues. What some faculty can more easily engage is profoundly difficult given contingent faculty working conditions. And sadly they point out that "institutions do not go too far out of their way to help adjunct faculty connect to the institution or to other faculty. Often, the impetus is placed on the adjunct faculty" (p. 66, this volume).

It is this lack of institutional support that this very book challenges by suggesting that higher education institutions should take on the responsibility of supporting and providing professional development for adjunct faculty. To fill this gap, the book offers new empirical research by reviewing the results of a survey of faculty developers to uncover exemplary stories of adjunct faculty development so that "we can deepen our own work and encourage others to do the same" (p. 4, this volume). The results point to key areas for faculty developers to examine to better support adjunct faculty. I highlight a few of these findings to demonstrate the value of this book. First, they identify how few faculty developers know if their campuses are unionized and suggest that a better understanding of academic unions could benefit these professionals. Second, they describe the importance of making professional development accessible in terms of timing and format—online options, for example. The survey also points out the importance of incentives for helping adjuncts to participate in professional development.

Third, this book provides exemplary practices from different institutions to help leaders addressed some of the survey. Like the adjunct voices section, they present stories from campuses of support for adjuncts—often by adjunct faculty themselves. For example,

Kirkland Community College established an adjunct faculty advisory committee that helps to develop the professional development programming and identify gaps in the professional development needs of adjuncts. Adjuncts from across the institution serve on the advisory committee. The group has helped to create orientation, and ongoing survey of adjunct faculty, and worked on inclusion by inviting contingent faculty to more events.

Throughout the chapters there is a common return to the idea that community needs to be restored to the professoriate. They outline an ambitious agenda of work for academic leaders to truly reinvent higher education so that adjuncts are treated as professionals; embraced as part of the faculty community; and moved from the margins, to be at the center where they belong.

Adrianna Kezar
Professor
University of Southern California
Director of the Delphi Project on the
Changing Faculty and Student Success
www.thechangingfaculty.org

SERIES FOREWORD

New Faculty Majority (NFM): The National Coalition for Adjunct and Contingent Equity was established in 2009 for one purpose: to focus on resolving the economic, ethical, political, and educational crises created by the shift to a predominantly contingent faculty workforce in higher education. The shift has occurred over decades, and it has led to an institutionalization of attitudes and policies toward contingent faculty members and toward faculty work more generally that must be described as counterproductive at best, exploitative at worst. By denying basic professional working conditions and opportunities for professional growth to faculty members without whom, ironically, higher education could not function, college and university leaders harm students and undermine the common good. Faculty working conditions are student learning conditions, so when faculty are not supported—not provided basic supports from offices to access to professional development—students are not supported. Similarly, when contingent faculty do not have academic freedom protections to ensure that they can challenge students and maintain high academic standards, they cannot fully carry out their duty to educate students to be active, responsible, discerning, and courageous citizens.

This series gives members of the academic community an opportunity to wrestle with these vexing, critical issues and to explore real-world, practical, and ethical solutions. It invites different audiences to be challenged and inspired to think; collaborate; and yes, to argue, in a way that is true to the diversity of experience that shapes us. Most important, this series highlights the voices and perspectives of contingent faculty themselves, so that all members of the higher education community committed to quality and equity can work toward these goals with integrity and in good faith.

NFM's objective from the beginning was to create a broad coalition of constituencies including faculty, students, parents, staff, administrators, labor activists, higher education organizations, and community members who would engage in inside/outside education and advocacy. Early in its existence, NFM realized that the project it had taken on was daunting in the same way that the crisis of climate change is so frustrating; namely, there was significant denial among people who should know better that the problem exists; it is man-made, and, therefore, it requires intentional, dedicated, and honest attention and effort to correct. This series is one important part of the effort to ensure that the climate of higher education is always as conducive to justice as it is to success.

Maria Maisto
President, New Faculty Majority

ACKNOWLEDGMENTS

We want to acknowledge the Delphi Center for Teaching and Learning at the University of Louisville for the support we received in the completion of this project.

Introduction

Marie Kendall Brown and Roy Fuller

The Need to Support Adjunct Faculty

When we think about the words *college* and *university*, images of ebullient students and scholarly professors are often the first to come to mind. Higher education institutions cannot function without faculty and without students, but the context in which faculty teach and conduct research has changed dramatically over the past few decades. Until recently, one change that has gone practically unnoticed by the general public is the increasing use of adjunct faculty members to perform the key educational function of teaching. National media attention of recent events such as the 2013 death of Margaret Mary Vojtko, a longtime adjunct faculty member at Duquesne University, and the subsequent revelation of her poverty status; a 2014 congressional hearing that offered a report on the status of adjunct faculty; and the growing advocacy and unionization movement have heightened awareness about the working conditions of this growing segment of higher education educators. In fact, adjunct faculty now compose the largest segment of the academic workforce (National Center for Education Statistics, 2015).

In his seminal book *The Courage to Teach*, Parker Palmer (2007) noted the importance of community for those who teach:

> The growth of any craft depends on shared practice and honest dialogue among the people who do it. We grow by private trial and error, to be sure—but our willingness to try, and fail, as individuals is severely limited when we are not supported by a community that encourages such risks. (p. 144)

Unfortunately, many adjunct faculty work in isolation. Because of evening or weekend teaching schedules, adjunct faculty may rarely, if ever, encounter colleagues and are thus not connected to a professional community. Palmer's observations about the *critical role that community and shared practice play with respect to professional development* are the driving forces that shape this book.

Over the past several decades, many colleges and universities have established centers for teaching and learning or other structures to support faculty professional development. Standard programming topics include instructional design, pedagogical techniques and strategies, and teaching with technology. Although full-time faculty typically have access to these opportunities, adjunct faculty are often left out because of scheduling conflicts, lack of awareness, or outright exclusion.

Shared practice happens when faculty developers organize and offer trainings or when colleagues gather to discuss, share strategies, and problem solve a challenge they face in the classroom. Sharing practice is what happens when individuals are connected to communities of practice. For many adjunct faculty, such opportunities are few and far between. We argue that colleges and universities must offer opportunities for professional development and community to *all* faculty members, especially those who serve in an adjunct capacity, in order to enhance teaching effectiveness and student success for all.

As the ranks of adjunct faculty have grown, professional development opportunities have lagged behind (Kezar & Gehrke, 2013). Those engaged in educational research investigate how learning can best be promoted, and many evidence-based instructional practices have been identified. The field of faculty development actively disseminates and translates this research to practice. Yet, many adjunct faculty continue to work in the shadows, and their needs for professional development and community are unmet. In this book, we share the stories of adjunct faculty who have sought and found or created professional development opportunities—and thus communities of shared practice—despite their marginalized status. Framing questions for our work here include the following:

- Who are adjunct faculty? What is known about the demographics of this growing and increasingly diverse population of educators?
- What unique challenges do adjunct faculty face with respect to institutional support for teaching and professional development?
- Where have adjunct faculty found or created communities of support? What are the characteristics of effective support for adjunct faculty?
- What can deans, chairs, course coordinators, and others in higher education administration do to support adjunct faculty professional development related to teaching?

As faculty developers in a center for teaching and learning at a research-intensive university, we have provided adjunct faculty professional development offerings for some time. In fact, our longest running program is the Part-Time Faculty Institute, which has been ongoing since 2005 (Hutti, Rhodes, Allison, & Lauterbach, 2007). Over the past few years, we have expanded our range of opportunities for adjunct faculty, and we have seen firsthand the impact this support has had on those who participate. Although maintaining the quality and relevance of our programs is a central goal, we also became aware of the importance of meeting another need: a place of community. Although the lack of community may be understood as an ongoing issue for some full-time faculty, it is particularly acute for adjunct faculty.

Schedule-induced isolation not only affects the ability of adjunct faculty to connect with other faculty but also can limit the ability of faculty developers to connect this population with professional development opportunities. Staffing and resource limitations may mean that it is not feasible to offer time-appropriate offerings. To better understand what we ourselves have experienced in our professional practice, we surveyed faculty developers who—like us—work with this population, either by offering programs specifically for adjunct faculty or through intentional outreach efforts. Many of our respondents described how limited resources and organizational attitudes that devalue the contributions of adjunct faculty have impeded their work. In addition, faculty developers who want to reach out to adjunct faculty often find that communication can be a challenge (Kezar & Maxey, 2012). Many institutions do not even *know* who the adjunct faculty are on their campuses. Worse, many adjunct faculty do not have reliable access to e-mail.

Although articles written by adjunct faculty about the adjunct experience may be found in journals and periodicals devoted to coverage of higher education, awareness of the increasing use of adjunct faculty and their working conditions continues to remain in the shadows of public awareness. Efforts to meet the needs of adjunct faculty continue to lag far behind at most institutions of higher education. For this reason, we are highlighting the stories of adjunct faculty and faculty developers who have offered or taken advantage of found professional development opportunities. To accomplish this goal, we put out a call for adjunct faculty to share their stories. We solicited submissions on the theme of community and were pleased to find adjunct faculty who not only found community in traditional professional development programs but also created their own communities of practice in innovative ways. We were also pleased to receive stories from faculty developers who are or who have been adjunct faculty, making them uniquely positioned to understand and serve this population.

Organization of This Book

Adjunct Faculty Voices contains two primary parts. In the first part of the book, we offer a current view of adjunct faculty, including demographics, working conditions, and efforts to advocate and organize adjunct labor. In chapter 1, we set the stage by describing the numerous types of adjunct faculty and explicating the shared challenges they face. For example, adjunct faculty are frequently offered the least desirable classes from the perspective of full-time faculty. At the same time, evening and weekend courses may be preferable for adjunct faculty who have other employment or needs that necessitate evening or weekend work. By choice or necessity, therefore, adjunct faculty may have limited opportunities to develop contacts and community with fellow faculty members. Chapter 1 also explores the demographics of adjunct faculty and builds on the work of Gappa and Leslie (1993) by proposing an updated typology of adjunct faculty. Surveys of adjunct faculty have revealed that adjunct faculty are often excluded from department meetings, which gives them little say in decisions that affect them and is another lost opportunity for contact with colleagues (Kezar & Maxey, 2014). In our own faculty development work with faculty across the disciplines, this story has been repeated numerous times. We also examine current trends in adjunct advocacy and organization. Chapters 2 through 6 feature selections from our adjunct faculty contributors who have elected to share their own experiences with seeking and finding opportunities for professional development and community.

Chapter 7 begins the second half of our work. In it, we share our analysis of findings from our survey of adjunct faculty development. The goal of that survey was to uncover exemplary stories of adjunct faculty development so that we can deepen our own work and encourage others do the same. Accordingly, chapters 8 through 13 feature selections related to planning and implementing programs in support of adjunct faculty. We characterize these as examples of best practices from the field. Our final chapter summarizes what we have learned about supporting adjunct faculty and offers suggestions and recommendations, both small and large in scope, for anyone committed to supporting the success of adjunct faculty.

Timely, responsive, and quality faculty development plays a vital role in the success of all faculty—regardless of employment status—and thus affects the success of institutions of higher education. If we continue to underserve the professional development needs of the largest segment of the higher education workforce, it will have consequences for institutions that are facing increasing scrutiny in regard to student academic success. We hope that the stories presented here will encourage administrators and faculty leaders to work with and for your adjunct faculty colleagues in new ways. If you are an adjunct faculty member, we hope you will be inspired by the stories included herein. If you are a faculty developer, we hope this work opens new avenues of programming relative to those who, we have found in our own experience, are most receptive of your help and attention.

References

Gappa, J., & Leslie, D. (1993). *The invisible faculty*. San Francisco, CA: Jossey-Bass.

Hutti, M., Rhodes, G., Allison, J., & Lauterbach, E. (2007). The Part-Time Faculty Institute: Strategically designed and continually assessed. In R. E. Lyons (Ed.), *Best practices for supporting adjunct faculty* (pp. 31–48). Bolton, MA: Anker.

Kezar, A., & Gehrke, S. (2013). Creating a high-quality place to teach, learn, and work. *Peer Review, 15*(3), 8–12.

Kezar, A., & Maxey, D. (2012). Missing from the institutional data picture: Non-tenure-track faculty. *New Directions for Institutional Research, 2012*(155), 47–65. doi:10.1002/ir.20021

Kezar, A., & Maxey, D. (2014). Troubling ethical lapses: The treatment of contingent faculty. *Change, 46*(4), 34–37. doi:10.1080/00091383.2014.925761

National Center for Education Statistics. (2015). Characteristics of postsecondary faculty. Retrieved from http://nces.ed.gov/programs/coe/indicator_cuf.asp

Palmer, P. (2007). *The courage to teach*. San Francisco, CA: Jossey-Bass.

Part One

Who Are Adjunct Faculty?

1

A Portrait of Adjunct Faculty

Marie Kendall Brown, Roy Fuller, and Kimberly Smith

Current Changes in Higher Education

The idyllic English-inspired model of a residential liberal arts education designed to "cultivate the life of the mind" and delivered by student-centered faculty in a pastoral setting has been replaced by the massification of higher education and a climate of scarcity, competition, and disengagement. The pressures facing American higher education in the twenty-first century are well documented. These include diminished public support, declining federal and state revenue, increasing expenditures, dropping enrollments, growing competition, and new instructional delivery methods. At many institutions, these pressures necessitate limited or stagnant salary increases, hiring freezes, and reductions in resources. As Austin and Gamson (1983) noted more than 30 years ago, "In the face of rising costs, public demands for accountability, and a tight labor market, the collegial structure of colleges and universities is fragmenting" (p. 1). We argue that productive and constructive collegial relationships, idea exchange, intellectual support and challenge, and a shared commitment to student learning and success can unite diverse faculty and create *esprit de corps*, the hallmark of a vibrant, successful, and motivated profession, especially in times of turbulence and change.

For many faculty, however, work-life quality has suffered as the expectation for securing research funding has increased and the resources and administrative support with which to conduct the three-pronged functions of research, teaching, and service have diminished. As professionals with specialized disciplinary knowledge and research skills, individual faculty members vary widely in how they allocate their time. Factors such as institutional type (e.g., two-year college, public, private, research), discipline, age, and career stage shape individual faculty workloads. However, rather than focus on nurturing collegial relationships, enhancing one's teaching contributions through professional development, or engaging in scholarly teaching practices, faculty today may be more likely to make the prudent decision to disengage from their students to focus on the research, funding, and publications for which they are rewarded and recognized.

Sadly, little has changed in the decades since Austin and Gamson (1983) noted that faculty work life is characterized by role conflict, ambiguous demands, heavy workloads, long hours, excessive demands, too many discrete tasks, limited advancement opportunities, and flat salary curves. More recently, public scrutiny of the tenure system—and a broader sense that many faculty are disinterested in students and their learning—has led to heightened calls for accountability measures. Considered together, these external pressures may be overshadowing the intrinsic benefits, such as academic freedom, autonomy, and intellectual exchange, that make academic work life appealing in the first place.

It is true that the nature, demographics, and job stability of those who are increasingly responsible for teaching and advising today's college students are vastly different from the way they were in the past. Full-time ranked faculty positions are in decline. According to the American Association of University Professors (AAUP, 2016), "Over the past four decades, the proportion of the academic labor force holding full-time tenured positions has declined by 26 percent and the shareholding full-time tenure track positions has dropped by 50 percent" (para. 2). During the same period, reliance on part-time faculty has increased. According to Kezar and Holcombe (2015), 70% of faculty are now off the tenure track (both full- and part-time). Schuster and Finkelstein (2006) noted that these dramatic increases in part-time and non-tenure-track appointments have rendered the tenure system *less relevant* to increasing numbers of academics.

Many in higher education, including the AAUP, contend that the current state of affairs presents a systemic threat to higher education because the tenure system ensures job security and academic freedom and has played a key role in making American colleges and universities the best in the world (AAUP, 2016). Indeed, achieving tenure is a "coin of the realm" designation for full-time faculty that carries with it a rich set of benefits including lifelong employment, academic freedom, and leadership in institutional governance, curriculum decisions, hiring, promotion, and tenure. According to AAUP, the tenure system enables faculty to "take greater risks in instruction and research, which often yield improved educational experiences and outcomes" (para. 3); conversely, an increasing reliance on faculty members in part-time positions has "eroded student retention and graduation rates at many institutions" (AAUP, 2016, para. 2).

As Kezar and Holcombe (2015) noted, two models of faculty work now exist: research-oriented faculty with tenure or on the tenure track, and non-tenure-track, mostly part-time faculty. Ironically, it is these research-oriented faculty members with tenure, or who are on the tenure track, who determine how instructional faculty are selected, hired, assigned, and valued at the department and institution levels. As access to higher education increases, institutions need skilled labor to teach large and diverse students in general education, entry-level, and large enrollment undergraduate courses. Employing part-time and adjunct faculty is cost-effective for cash-strapped institutions, and this segment of the academic workforce fulfills a critical instructional need. At the same time that they contribute in significant ways to fulfilling the academic mission of higher education, adjunct faculty have acquired second-class status because they typically do not bring in coveted research dollars. Their contributions are therefore marginalized to the "less profitable" areas of teaching, community engagement, and service (Kezar & Holcombe, 2015).

On the flipside of this "narrative of constraint" about faculty roles, O'Meara, LaPointe Terosky, and Neumann (2008) offered a counter narrative of "growth" whereby faculty adopt a generative view that holds on to learning and intellectual growth in the face of external pressures and financial constraint. Indeed, Henry Rosvosky (1980), in his book *The University: An Owner's Manual*, noted that learning and professional development is central to a faculty member's work, "The essence of academic life is the opportunity—indeed, the demand—for continual investment in oneself. It is a unique chance for a lifetime of building and renewing intellectual capital" (p. 161). The trouble is that external forces have deeply altered academic professionalism with as yet unknown consequences. As Kezar and Holcombe (2015) noted, many in higher education are genuinely concerned about "the growing reliance on contingent labor and its implications for institutions, the ability of all faculty members to do their jobs, and the future of academic professionalism" (para. 16). Given this challenging frame, who are these isolated, marginalized, and invisible adjunct and part-time faculty? And how might understanding their circumstances and professional development needs help those of us in higher education better support their success as educators?

Demographics and Types of Adjunct Faculty

Adjunct faculty now compose the largest single category of educators in the higher education workforce, constituting approximately 50% of all college faculty. Hard data regarding demographics and working conditions remain difficult to obtain because of numerous factors (Coalition on the Academic Workforce, 2012; Kezar & Maxey, 2012), which may explain why data on adjunct faculty have been scarce. Cross and Goldenberg (2009) described a lack of uniformity concerning terms used for *adjunct faculty, decentralized hiring,* and *inconsistent* (or a lack of) *standards* and policies in regard to reporting institutional data. Kezar and Maxey (2012) added additional factors: (a) a lack of prioritization in regard to reporting proper data concerning non-tenure-track faculty and (b) a fear of unionization, which drives some administrations to engage in data collection to support the case for collective bargaining. These challenges, along with the end of funding for the National Study of Postsecondary Faculty in 2004, mean that other surveys and organizations have attempted to address the lack of data on adjunct faculty. The 2010 Coalition on the Academic Workforce (CAW) study, *A Portrait of Part-Time Faculty Members*, offers a snapshot of adjunct faculty drawing on a self-selected population of over 20,000 contingent faculty (CAW, 2012). Because it is one of the larger recent surveys of adjunct faculty, we use its findings as a baseline for the portrait offered next.

Demographics

Females accounted for 61.9% of survey respondents, and nearly 90% of respondents who reported their race or ethnicity identified themselves as White. By way of comparison, the National Center for Education Statistics 2009 Fall Staff Survey reported 51.6% of adjuncts are female, with 81.9% classified as White. Although gender did not emerge as a determining factor in regard to pay per course, the CAW report did raise questions about the impact of race on pay, with respondents self-identifying as Black reporting earning up to 25% less per course (CAW, 2012).

Although noting that further analysis is needed in regard to age variability of adjuncts, the CAW report observed that 70.8% of the respondents were between the ages of 36 and 65 years, with those between the ages of 26 and 35 years composing 19.3%, those older than 65 years registering at 9%, and those younger than 25 years registering at 1% (CAW, 2012). This finding challenges the assumption that part-time faculty are either recent graduates taking first steps toward academic employment or older professionals who are retired and now teach as a second, part-time career. Indeed, the CAW (2012) reported, "73.3% of respondents indicated that they considered teaching in higher education their primary employment" (p. 9). Although the term *adjunct* may accurately describe people's status within a single institution, it does not accurately capture the reality of their employment status or how they themselves view their work.

As to institution type and subject taught, the CAW report found that 38.5% of courses were taught at associate-granting institutions followed by 29.2% at Carnegie-classified master's institutions. Respondents taught in 35 disciplinary categories, with the humanities representing the largest percentage of the courses taught (44%), followed by courses taught in professional fields (20.5%). English language and literature made up 16.4% of courses taught, the single largest discipline represented, which is reflective of most English departments' dependence on adjunct faculty (CAW, 2012).

Academic credentials held by those respondents featured in the CAW report are as follows: 40.2% held a master's degree, 30.4% held a doctoral degree, 16.7% held a professional or other terminal degree, and 7.0% had all but their dissertation (CAW, 2012). By comparison, the Just-in-Time Professor (House Committee on Education and the Workforce, 2014) report found that 55% of respondents held a doctoral degree, with 35% holding a master's degree and less than 2% with industry experience or a terminal-degree equivalent.

One factor needing further research is the desire of adjunct faculty for full-time academic employment. Earlier work by Gappa and Leslie (1993) suggested that part-time faculty were generally satisfied with their employment status. This claim was supported by Antony and Valadez (2002), whose conclusion bears repeating, as it challenges traditional assumptions: "Specifically, instead of being largely disenchanted with their status as part-time faculty, these individuals are in fact engaged in the kind of work they enjoy—work that brings them a degree of satisfaction" (pp. 54–55). Although these researchers noted that further studies are needed to explore whether the dimensions of satisfaction are the same for part-time and full-time faculty, these claims have countered the prevailing assumption that part-time faculty are not satisfied (see also Gappa, 2000; Leslie & Gappa, 2002).

Caution should be used in making any bold claims relating to part-time faculty satisfaction, because few studies exist, and even fewer distinguish between faculty who might be classified as "voluntary part-time"—those who desire part-time positions—and "involuntary part-time"—those who are seeking full-time academic appointments (Eagan, Jaeger, & Grantham, 2015, p. 452). When such distinctions have been made, it is possible to conclude that involuntary part-time faculty reported significantly lower levels of job satisfaction when compared to voluntary part-time faculty (Maynard & Joseph, 2008). Although the previous statement seems obvious on its face, the variability in faculty appointments and the diversity of part-time faculty are factors that are not always considered by researchers and academic administrators. Research on part-time faculty job satisfaction has begun to recognize that as a factor or category for exploration, *satisfaction* is a nuanced term. In contrast to claims that part-time faculty are more satisfied than commonly thought, recent studies have suggested this is not the case. Although they do indicate that part-time faculty are satisfied with their teaching role, they are concerned about matters of equitable treatment by colleagues and the institutions that employ them. To speak of satisfaction in isolation, without noting other factors relating to academic employment such as salary and working conditions, has the potential for offering a skewed picture of adjunct working conditions.

One factor that sheds light on the nature of adjunct employment is the question of desirability of full-time employment by adjunct faculty. Although many have accepted Leslie and Gappa's (2002) claim that "only a small fraction of part-timers are eagerly seeking full-time positions" (p. 65), such claims are coming under increasing scrutiny. Maynard and Joseph (2008) reported that approximately 27% of respondents indicated a preference for a full-time teaching position. In their 2014 study of 405 community college faculty members, Kramer, Gloeckner, and Jacoby found that 49% of respondents indicated a preference for a full-time teaching position. Townsend and Hauss (2002) reported 67% of respondents stated that the reason they teach part-time is their inability to find a full-time teaching position. In a study of part-time faculty at one community college, Jacoby (2005) stated, "The data suggest that discouragement increases both with age and experience" (p. 143), suggesting that career stage needs to be taken into account when overall satisfaction is the question. The CAW (2012) report found "a significant desire on the part of part-time faculty respondents to move into full-time tenure-track positions" (p. 9), with 29.6% of respondents indicating they were currently seeking a full-time tenure-track position, and another 20.1% indicating they intended to do so.

Research continues to be mixed on how many part-time faculty desire full-time employment. Muncaster (2011), using the 2004 National Study of Postsecondary Faculty data, concluded, "The stereotype of part-time faculty being a group who, in general, would prefer full-time employment in academia is not supported by these data" (p. 35). Yet, Eagan and colleagues (2015), using the Higher Education Research Institute's 2010–2011 Faculty Survey, found that "73% of part-time faculty in this sample were identified as being underemployed or involuntarily employed part-time—working in part-time appointments but desiring or seeking full-time academic positions" (p. 463). Satisfaction gaps also emerged between White and non-White faculty, "with White faculty reporting significantly higher levels of workplace satisfaction" (p. 470) even as they called for additional research to explain this finding. A significant satisfaction gap was identified between part-time faculty working at private colleges and universities who rated "themselves as significantly more satisfied compared to their colleagues at public universities" (p. 471), though the authors did not offer any explanation for this gap. The most significant conclusion drawn by Eagan and colleagues (2015) was that in regard to overall adjunct faculty satisfaction, "part-time faculty in this study were not satisfied with relationships with administrators and colleagues" (p. 472), which negatively affected satisfaction with other job factors. The significance of this finding cannot be overstated in regard to the possibility of improving the satisfaction levels of part-time faculty, as improving relationships between administrators and colleagues could be accomplished without additional financial resources.

Toutkoushian and Bellas (2003), using data from the 1993 National Survey of Part-Time Faculty, found that 22.5% of *all* faculty prefer part-time employment, with women being 6% more likely to prefer part-time employment—though among faculty already employed part-time, "there was little gender difference in their preference for part-time employment" (p. 182). Toutkoushian and Bellas (2003) measured three aspects of job satisfaction: overall job satisfaction, satisfaction with job benefits, and satisfaction with salary. They found that part-time faculty were "much less satisfied than full-time faculty with their benefits" (pp. 189–191) even as part-time faculty were "more satisfied with their jobs overall" (p. 191). These findings are consistent with those from the National Survey of Part-Time Adjunct Faculty, which found that although part-time faculty job satisfaction is fairly high, the results are fairly evenly split when it comes to those who prefer part-time teaching (50%) and those who would prefer full-time teaching jobs (47%), increasing to 60% for those younger than age 50 years (AFT Higher Education, 2010).

Feldman and Turnley (2001) examined how career stage affected part-time faculty's attitudes toward their status and offered two conclusions relevant to this discussion. First, "the most positive aspects of non-tenure-track jobs involve the work itself and relationships with professional colleagues" (p. 12), thus supporting other studies that have found that part-time faculty have a high level of satisfaction with the work itself. Second, in regard to the specific variable of *career stage*, defined in this study by age of partici-pants, with *early career* defined as persons in their 20s, *mid career* as persons in their 30s and 40s, and *late career* as persons in their 50s, Feldman and Turnley (2001) found, "Adjunct faculty in late career demonstrated more positive job attitudes and work behaviors than adjunct faculty in early or mid-career. Adjunct faculty in early career were most disappointed by the lack of advancement opportunities they perceived in their non-tenure-track jobs" (p. 12). Although acknowledging that measures of career stage based on age rely on approximations, Feldman and Turnley's findings suggest that career stage is a factor that should be included when questions of adjunct faculty job satisfaction arise.

A final factor to note in regard to whether part-time faculty are satis-fied with their part-time status may be revealed by noting the numbers of institutions where they teach. Street, Maisto, Merves, and Rhoades (2012) found that more than half (54%) of 500 respondents teach in more than one institution, with 29% teaching in two institutions, 11% teaching in three institutions, and 6% teaching in four institutions. The House Committee on Education and the Workforce (2014), working off data provided by 217 respondents who offered information on the number of institutions at which they taught, found similar findings and noted, "48 percent taught at two institutions, 27 percent taught at three institutions, and 13 percent taught at four or more institutions" (p. 13). A 2014 study at George Mason University also found that significant percentages of the university's adjunct faculty were employed as adjunct faculty at more than one university, "with 26 percent employed at two, 8 percent employed at three, and 2 percent employed at four or more" (Allison, Lynn, & Hoverman, 2014, p. 19). One conclusion to be drawn from such findings is that for a significant percentage of part-time faculty, full-time employment is both desirable and difficult to obtain and that many part-time faculty are unable to make ends meet by teaching for a single institution. Comments submitted to the House Committee on Education and the Workforce identified one major drawback to part-time employment at multiple institutions. As one respondent stated, "The commuting was expensive and time-consuming; during one period, I drove nearly 100 miles a day around a triangle from my home to two jobs and back again" (House Committee on Education and the Workforce, 2014, p. 14). These reports suggest that the phenomenon of the "freeway flier" is real and may account for a larger percentage of part-time faculty than previously recognized.

Typologies of Adjunct Faculty

Part-time faculty are a diverse group of educators. When educators are presented with a diverse population, the natural scholarly impulse is to develop a typology in an effort to bring order to the chaos. Muncaster (2011) briefly traced the development of typologies for part-time faculty, noting the first typology was found in Tuckman's (1978) article "Who Is Part-Time in Academe?" in the *Bulletin of the American Association of University Professors*. Building on Tuckman's work, Gappa and Leslie's (1993) *The Invisible Faculty* is the second typology and has become the standard adjunct typology model. Their categories and their definitions include the following: (a) *career enders*—retired or preretired educators who are in transition from established careers; (b) *specialist, expert, or professional*—those who come from a wide range of fields and careers who typically have a full-time career outside academia; (c) *aspiring academics*—those who hope for full-time involvement as an academic (for Gappa and Leslie, this category included part-time faculty with terminal degrees who desire full-time academic careers and all-but-disseration doctoral students); and (d) *freelancers*—those whose preference is for work at several different part-time occupations, of which teaching is only one. In two subsequent studies, Gappa and Leslie maintained and defended their original categories, as well as their claims that most adjunct faculty have full or near full-time nonteaching employment, and maintained that the percentage of "freeway fliers" and aspiring academics (at least in the community college context) is lower than generally perceived in the media (Leslie & Gappa, 1997, 2002).

Gappa and Leslie's typology provided evidence of the diversity and work conditions of adjunct faculty. To be beneficial, a typology must be both accurate and not overly complicated, as the whole point is to capture a complex population with as few categories as possible while still doing justice to the diverse population in question. In the case of any typology of adjunct faculty, one challenge is to accurately represent the career arc of an individual faculty member, who may be classified under several types depending on his or her career and/or life stage. Schwartz (2007) noted this limitation in regard to his own experience, observing, "Many part-timers, I later discovered, do not fit neatly into one of the categories of *Aspiring Academics, Career Enders, Freelancers,* and *Specialist/Expert/Professional,* while others seem to move between categories over time" (p. 243, emphasis in original). Certainly many adjunct faculty known to the authors of this publication would concur with Schwartz's observation.

To further refine Gappa and Leslie's typology, researchers have proposed additional types. Muncaster (2011) found it desirable to add two additional categories to Gappa and Leslie's original four: *road scholars* and *minimalists.* Faculty who teach frequently at two or more different institutions and are teaching at least five classes are labeled *road scholars,* whereas *minimalists* are those who are not retired and teach at most two courses per year at only one institution. Minimalists also do not hold another position outside higher education and do not have an interest in becoming a full-time faculty member (Muncaster, 2011). More study would be required to answer questions about this minimalists group, such as the following: How do they support themselves teaching only two courses a year? What other aspects of their profile might reveal additional support, such as a working spouse?

The road scholars type was nuanced by Gappa and Leslie (1993) as "freeway fliers," though they did not incorporate it as a separate type, preferring to place this set of adjunct faculty under their aspiring academic category, even as they acknowledged the freeway flier form of employment "is probably more common in large metropolitan areas" and called for further study of this type "with particular emphasis on geography" (p. 49). Muncaster (2011) found that approximately 10% of respondents could be classified as road scholars, with minimalists accounting for 4.6% (p. 79). Johnson (2015) interrogated Gappa and Leslie's original four categories and found that additional categories were necessary to more accurately capture the current reality of all adjuncts, as well as the numerous roles a single adjunct might hold, both over the span of a career and at the same time.

As opposed to generating additional categories to create a more accurate typology, researchers may find it more advantageous to further define the current types by adding additional traits to the categories. For example, to capture the reality of multicampus employment, could we say that a person can be in any of the previously mentioned four or six categories and then note whether such a person teaches at one campus or more than one? Also, rather than putting the emphasis on primary employment status, as the Gappa and Leslie model does, might we note that these categories are better understood in relation to one's age or career stage? Thus, one might be a freelancer as a recent PhD at any age or as someone moving into a second career. Following up on the work of Maynard and Joseph (2008), which added information regarding whether a person is a voluntary or involuntary part-time faculty, would be advantageous, as this factor affects job satisfaction. Might surveys better capture the satisfaction factor by more fully exploring the many factors that contribute to that state, thus more accurately capturing the number of part-time faculty who, although reporting high levels of satisfaction in regard to teaching, nonetheless are not satisfied with their transitory employment status? The following categories combine an updated version of the Gappa and Leslie types (supplemented by Muncaster, 2011, and others) with the previously mentioned variables.

Voluntary Part-Time Faculty

The following categories or types are related because of the voluntary nature of one's choosing to teach in a less than full-time capacity. This choice may be due to career stage, full-time employment elsewhere, or educational status.

- *Graduate students:* These are individuals who are working toward a graduate or terminal degree and who teach in a part-time capacity either because it is part of their financial aid package or because it is their choice to gain experience. They might be considered "hopefuls" or "aspiring academics," as they may be anticipating full-employment as a teacher.
- *Outside specialists:* These are persons who are employed full-time in a position outside of academia but who teach in a part-time capacity. Such are experts or professionals in their field and are sought out as teachers for their experience. They are not interested in full-time teaching.

- *Voluntary freelancers:* These are persons who choose part-time teaching and combine it with other part-time employment opportunities. This category also includes persons who prefer part-time teaching and have no other employment because of family obligations or choice.
- *Career enders:* These persons are those who have retired from a full-time career, perhaps as a full-time academic, but who now seek to teach in a part-time capacity. Some desire to keep current in their field of expertise, others have a love of teaching, and still others see this as a transition to full retirement.

Although these four types vary in regard to career stage and motivation, they seek and prefer part-time teaching. As Maynard and Joseph (2008) showed in their study of job satisfaction, adjuncts who were voluntarily part-time had a satisfaction level consistent with that of full-time faculty, and in some cases their emotional commitment to their academic institutions was higher than that of full-time faculty. We believe that these categories reflect this reality and if used for further studies would yield more accurate and useful data regarding adjunct faculty.

Involuntary Part-Time Faculty

As with the types delineated previously, these types also vary in career stage and motivation, but they share a desire for a full-time teaching:

- *Aspiring hopefuls:* These persons are those who have recently completed their degree and who are teaching part-time because that is the best opportunity available. These persons are at the beginning of an academic career but have not found a full-time position in the academy.
- *Involuntary freelancers:* These persons are traditionally understood as those who teach part-time and combine that with other part-time nonteaching positions. This description is true for some but may also include those who might be labeled *road scholars*, who combine part-time teaching at more than one institution into something that resembles full-time work, though without benefits.

Although these categories will not capture every demographic trait of part-time faculty, we believe that these categories offer a more complete picture that can inform both the general public and the academic administrators charged with overseeing the hiring and working conditions of part-time faculty. In particular, the acknowledgment of the voluntary and involuntary part-time status would be a significant additional factor for future surveys and research to explore, as this factor affects both job satisfaction and how institutions might best support adjunct faculty. Though questions remain as to the percentage of adjunct faculty who are involuntarily part-time, Johnson's (2015) survey found that somewhere between 50% and 75% may fall into this category. With the numbers of adjunct faculty being employed in higher education continuing to increase, a more precise typology that goes beyond career stage and employment outside of academia will better serve both administrators and faculty developers who seek to support and advocate on behalf of adjunct faculty.

Working Conditions and Issues Facing Adjunct Faculty

As noted previously, working conditions for adjuncts vary widely depending on one's career stage and reason for becoming an adjunct professor and on the institution(s) one teaches for. Some studies have found that most adjuncts are satisfied with their positions and are not seeking full-time positions (Gappa & Leslie, 1993); however, at the other extreme, there are professors like Margaret Mary Vojtko. Vojtko taught as an adjunct faculty member at Duquesne University for over 25 years. She was still working into her 80s because of a meager salary and lack of benefits that made it unfeasible for her to retire (Hightower, 2014; Kezar & Maxey, 2014). Vojtko, who suffered from cancer and a heart condition, attempted to unionize along with other Duquesne adjunct faculty members for better pay and health insurance, but the university refused (and continues to refuse) to recognize the union (Anderson, 2013; Kezar & Maxey, 2014). During Vojtko's last few years at Duquesne, the university gradually reduced her teaching load from three courses per semester to two, and then to one, reducing her annual income to less than $10,000 (Anderson, 2013; Hightower, 2014). In the spring of 2013, she was informed that her contract would not be renewed. As an adjunct, she received no severance package. On September 1 of that same year, Vojtko died at the age of 83 years of a cardiac arrest (Anderson, 2013).

Following her death, Vojtko's story became a rallying cry for the national adjunct community (Anderson, 2013). Adjunct professors across the country pointed to this account as a vivid example of academia's ill treatment of adjuncts. Many have argued that Duquesne should have done more to "save" Vojtko. Whether or not Vojtko's death could have been prevented, it is possible that had Duquesne recognized the adjunct union and provided adjuncts with better pay and benefits, the end of her life may have looked very different. Vojtko's story prompts important questions about the working conditions of adjuncts. Does the typical adjunct faculty member experience conditions as extreme as those experienced by Vojtko? If so, what can be done about it?

Because of the diversity among adjunct faculty, it is difficult to paint a characteristic picture of working conditions for the entire population. For instance, AFT Higher Education's 2010 national survey of 500 part-time and adjunct faculty found that relatively equal numbers of adjuncts have annual incomes below $50,000 and exceeding $100,000. This is influenced by the fact that 38% of adjuncts surveyed had nonteaching jobs in addition to their adjunct role (AFT Higher Education, 2010). The fact that some adjunct professors are well off should not distract from the situation of many adjuncts who are struggling to make ends meet. Nationwide, contingent faculty earn an average salary of just $2,700 per class (Allison et al., 2014). Twenty-five percent of part-time faculty and their families are enrolled in government assistance programs (Jacobs, Perry, & MacGillvary, 2015). The typical contingent faculty member has accrued $50,000 to $60,000 of debt from student loans and may have little hope of repaying these debts on an adjunct salary (Kezar & Maxey, 2014). Job security is also a concern for adjuncts hired via at-will employment practices that provide no guarantees of an appointment the next semester (Rhoades, 2012).

Hiring Practices

The discussion around the working conditions of part-time faculty tends to focus on salary and benefits, but there are other ways that institutions can support adjunct professors. Institutions are largely failing to provide adjuncts with what is needed to perform their job successfully. A basic need of faculty is time to prepare for one's course—time that is denied to those who are hired just before the start of classes, a predominant hiring practice for part-time faculty (Rhoades, 2012). At George Mason University, contingent faculty were asked to report the least amount of lead time they were given to prepare for a course in the spring 2013 semester. One third of the 241 respondents had less than two weeks to prepare for at least one of their courses, whereas one fourth had less than one week (Allison et al., 2014). These "just-in-time" hiring practices manage to put a teacher in the classroom in time for the first class period, but that teacher may have insufficient time to prepare for the course and may miss out on opportunities to interact with students prior to the start of course (Street et al., 2012). Faculty who are hired with little notice may be unable to place their textbook orders in time for the bookstore to stock them, thus students are unable to obtain their books before the semester begins. This can negatively affect students' views of the professor. In the words of one adjunct faculty member, "It makes me look sloppy and unprepared when the text isn't available" (Street et al., 2012). Adjunct faculty hired at the last minute are also unable to orient themselves to the text if they have not used it before, or they may select a textbook they have used previously that is not an ideal choice for the given course (Street et al., 2012).

Often, adjunct faculty members have not received their course assignments by the time students are registering for the upcoming semester. Some students want to take additional courses in later semesters from a faculty member that they particularly enjoyed; they may have benefited from the professor's teaching style or wish to further build a relationship with that professor. Not knowing what courses a faculty member will be assigned to creates difficulties for such students in planning their course schedule (Street et al., 2012). Arguably the most detrimental effect of just-in-time hiring practices is that faculty who have limited time to prepare for their course may be poorly positioned to incorporate innovative pedagogical methods into their teaching (Kezar & Maxey, 2014).

Access to Basic Resources and Teaching Support

Upon hire, adjuncts frequently find themselves without access to some of the basic resources they need to adequately perform their job. These include e-mail accounts, curriculum guidelines, library privileges, printers and copiers, software, technology support, and office space (Kezar & Maxey, 2014; Street et al., 2012). Adjuncts who have no office space or share office space with multiple instructors often find it difficult to have private conversations with students. Nevertheless, the institution may require that some issues be handled privately, such as when a student is struggling in the course (Street et al., 2012). Those who cannot copy materials or obtain needed software with department resources may cover these expenses themselves or may be deterred from using these materials altogether (Street et al., 2012). One survey conducted by Campaign for the Future of Higher Education and the New Faculty Majority Foundation asked 500 adjunct faculty about working conditions at their institutions (Street et al., 2012). Reporting on their appointments in which they received the *most* access to campus resources,

- 45% gained library privileges less than two weeks before the class start date,
- 34% received sample syllabi less than two weeks before the class start date,
- 32% received curriculum guidelines less than two weeks before the class start date,
- 21% never received curriculum guidelines, and
- 21% never obtained access to office space (Street et al., 2012).

Adjuncts may be denied a comprehensive orientation to the institution and opportunities for continued professional development. A study of 65 journalism programs found that 61% of programs surveyed did not offer any formal orientation for adjuncts (Abrams, 2006). Only 52.8% of contingent faculty members working at George Mason University in spring 2013 reported receiving an orientation to their academic department. Approximately 45% received a teaching orientation, and 31% received an orientation to human resources (Allison et al., 2014). Another study that surveyed 278 college deans found that nearly half the institutions in the sample lacked policies to promote mentoring and participation in professional development opportunities for adjunct faculty (Kezar & Gehrke, 2013). Despite the importance of ongoing teaching support for any faculty member, sources in the literature provide little information regarding the current state of professional development for adjuncts, especially as it extends beyond formal orientations. In an effort to address this gap in the literature, current practices and deficiencies in adjunct professional development are explored further throughout this book via the personal stories of adjunct faculty members, reported findings from our own study of faculty developers, and several accounts of model programs.

Voice in Governance

A lack of representation in departmental or institutional decision-making may also inhibit adjuncts from performing their jobs effectively by disconnecting them from their college or university. In Abrams's (2006) survey of journalism program administrators, 30% of institutions reported that adjunct faculty members were not invited to regular faculty meetings. Only 22% of responding programs said that adjuncts were allowed to vote on issues put before the faculty. On a positive note, 92% of respondents indicated that adjunct faculty were included in social events (Abrams, 2006). Still, missed opportunities to include adjuncts in departmental and institutional discussions have resulted in a tendency for adjunct faculty to feel invisible on their campuses. This is exemplified by the fact that their names may not be listed on course registrations; instead, registrations may list the instructor for adjunct-taught courses as simply "staff" (Street et al., 2012). Insufficient data collection by institutions on their adjunct faculty and a lack of opportunities for adjuncts to anonymously voice concerns about their working conditions further isolate adjuncts from the administrators who could improve those conditions (Kezar & Maxey, 2014; Leslie & Gappa, 1997). Fear that their contracts may not be renewed should they speak up about problems they are experiencing—in addition to a sense that administrators may not care what they have to say—may impose silence on these issues (Kezar & Maxey, 2014).

The Connection Between Adjunct Support and Student Learning

The false notion that instruction is something that occurs only in the classroom—neglecting the many instructional activities that take place before and outside of class—has contributed to the inadequate working conditions of many adjuncts across the nation (Street et al., 2012). Professors who are unable to perform their out-of-class responsibilities—such as planning their course, preparing materials, and communicating with students—are unable to teach effectively, and adjunct faculty are all too often placed in this difficult position. Of course, adjunct faculty can have positive impacts on student learning; hiring adjuncts offers a relatively inexpensive and flexible solution for maintaining or reducing class sizes, and many adjuncts bring specialized skills and expertise from professional experience outside academia, which tenured faculty may not have to offer (Leslie & Gappa, 1997). However, the disadvantages that adjunct faculty members face in comparison to tenured and tenure-track faculty inevitably have a negative impact on students by diminishing adjuncts' capacity to provide quality instruction and inhibiting their ability to be available to students outside the classroom (Rhoades, 2012).

Analyzing the responses of 17,914 faculty members from 130 institutions to the spring 2004 Faculty Survey of Student Engagement, Umbach (2007) found a negative association between part-time status and faculty performance related to undergraduate education. Part-time faculty used active and collaborative instructional techniques less frequently than tenured and tenure-track faculty. They were less likely to challenge their students, and they spent significantly less time preparing for class. Part-time and full-time contingent faculty were found to interact less often with students on both class-related and nonclass-related matters (Umbach, 2007). In another study of four-year institutions in one state system, researchers discovered that first-year students who took between 76% and 100% of their first-year classes with adjunct faculty members were significantly less likely to persist than students who took less than 25% of their classes with adjuncts (Jaeger, 2008).

Institutions often justify their reliance on poorly paid adjunct faculty as an economic necessity (Leslie & Gappa, 1997; Spector, 2013). Although tight budgets may be an understandable and unavoidable limitation, many of the previously noted concerns could be addressed with little or no additional allocation of resources. For instance, granting adjunct faculty earlier access to library resources, listing adjunct faculty members on registration sites or departmental websites, or including adjuncts in university or departmental decision-making should cost little to nothing (Street et al., 2012). Institutions should also recognize that the allocation of resources indicates where one's priorities lie (Kezar & Maxey, 2014). If student learning is truly a priority, institutions have an obligation to invest resources in the adjunct faculty members who now teach a majority of courses in U.S. institutions.

According to Terry Hartle, senior vice president of the American Council on Education, "Nobody forces someone to become an adjunct" ("Is Academia Suffering," 2014). Does this mean that adjunct faculty are to blame for their own problems? If adjuncts are unhappy with the terms and conditions of their employment, why do they not find a different career? By creating a surplus of PhDs, institutions themselves may play a role in perpetuating the reality of adjuncts who feel trapped in unsatisfactory circumstances. More students are encouraged to pursue careers in academia than there are tenure-track positions available ("Is Academia Suffering," 2014). Institutions have been criticized for taking advantage of inexpensive PhD student labor in order to enhance research and teaching capacity while rewarding these students with degrees that are likely neither to land them the secure full-time position in academia for which they set out nor to prepare them for positions outside academia ("The Disposable Academic," 2010). Even after new PhDs realize the reality of the job market in academia, they often decide not to change course because they feel ill prepared to perform any other career, because of their passion for teaching, or because of the significant time and financial resources they have invested in their education ("Is Academia Suffering," 2014).

Unionization and Support Organizations

With increasing awareness of the working conditions of adjunct faculty, the unionization movement has grown. Articles bearing titles such as "The Adjunct Revolt: How Poor Professors Are Fighting Back" (Segran, 2014), "Adjunct Advocacy: Contingent Faculty Members Are Demanding—and Getting—Better Working Conditions" (Schmidt, 2015), and "The Social Injustice Done to Adjunct Faculty: A Call to Arms" (Smith, 2015) reveal an increasing emphasis on organization. This represents a shift from merely lamenting the status of adjunct to a call to arms for organization, or what one activist labeled "from awfulizing to organizing" (Rhoades, 2015, p. 436). Gary Rhoades, a sociologist who has documented adjunct faculty unions, observed,

I have seen a shift in the consciousness of contingent activists, particularly among those most focused on organizing "adjunct" faculty working in (often multiple) part-time positions. The change is born of years, even decades of experience of extraordinary and increasingly exploitative working conditions and salaries. (Rhoades, 2015, pp. 435–436)

Increases in union organizing (and membership) among adjunct faculty is challenging the national narrative on unions, where membership in unions has declined since the early 1980s. Although overall union membership rates in the United States have declined from 20.1% in 1983 to 11.1% in 2015, the highest unionization rates can be found in education, training, library, and protective service occupations (Bureau of Labor Statistics, 2016). In fact, public sector workers have a union membership rate more than five times higher than that of private sector workers: 35.2% versus 6.7% (Bureau of Labor Statistics, 2016). Although there are challenges to knowing how many college faculty are covered by collectively bargained contracts, the number most often quoted is 386,000 from a study by Berry and Savaris (2012). Unions have historically been the tool used to address poor working conditions and low pay, factors widely seen as characterizing the adjunct experience. For this reason, it makes sense that union organizing has emerged in response to the ongoing dialogue about adjunct faculty.

Issues Pertaining to Unions in Academia

A number of philosophical and practical issues are relevant here. In *Unionization in the Academy*, DeCew (2003) grouped the arguments regarding the impact of unions under the following broad headings: (a) whether unions promote collegiality or adversity, (b) whether unions promote effectiveness or are a liability, (c) whether unions are needed because of the increasing corporate philosophy within higher education, and (d) arguments regarding the impact of unions on fundamental academic values such as faculty governance, collegiality, and academic freedoms. How does the unionization of tenure-line faculty relate to that of non-tenure-line faculty? How has the emergence of unions of contingent faculty on campuses where no faculty unions exist affected the relationship among the various categories of faculty? Issues surrounding unionization are part of the changing higher education environment and affects faculty of all types, administrators, students, and, most important, student learning.

Current Status of Unionization Efforts of Adjunct Faculty

How many adjunct faculty are covered by union negotiated contracts, which are typically known as *collective bargaining agreements* (CBAs)? The National Education Association's (NEA's) database of CBAs listed only five contracts for part-time-only bargaining units in the 1990s. As of 2012, the NEA database listed 57 contracts for part-time-only faculty (Dougherty, Rhoades, & Smith, 2014). Although these NEA databases are incomplete, as they do not list all CBAs, the overall number of part-time faculty covered under CBAs in 2012 was 147,019 (Dougherty et al., 2014). The National Center for the Study of Collective Bargaining in Higher Education and the Professions at Hunter College (drawing on its 2012 directory) put the number of unionized part-time faculty at 172,000 (Belkin & Korn, 2015), while New Faculty Majority (n.d.-a), a national adjunct advocacy organization founded in 2009, claimed that about 25% of part-time faculty in the United States are unionized. The total number of adjunct faculty in the United States is estimated to be in excess of 750,000 (National Center for Education Statistics, 2015).

As media interest in adjuncts has increased and as adjuncts have begun organizing themselves, the traditional unions for higher education faculty, such as the American Federation of Teachers and the AAUP, have begun to take notice. Unions new to the sector include the United Steelworkers; United Auto Workers; Newspaper Guild, Communications Workers of America; and Service Employees International Union (SEIU). SEIU has organized about 21,000 adjuncts nationwide (Dunn, 2014) and has focused much of its attention on organizing adjunct faculty in metropolitan areas (New Faculty Majority, n.d.-a). California is the state with the highest percentage of unionized part-time faculty, with "nearly 100 percent of part-time faculty in the three public systems . . . including all in the UC and CSU systems" (New Faculty Majority, n.d.-a, para. 2). A similar statewide effort to organize part-time faculty in Florida is the goal of the Adjunct Faculty Union (New Faculty Majority, n.d.-a). The Coalition of Contingent Academic Labor (COCAL), a national network of union activists and advocates, maintains that there are 22 states where active organizing is occurring (Berry & Worthen, 2014).

One primary measure of the impact of unionization for adjuncts is per-course remuneration (Dougherty et al., 2014). Although these organizing efforts focus on a wide range of issues pertinent to adjunct employment practices, from the impact of new education technologies and the Affordable Care Act to compensation for class cancellations and acknowledgment of nonteaching work assignments, per-course remuneration is perhaps the best documented. The 2010 CAW survey found that unionized adjuncts earned 25% more per course than nonunionized adjuncts, $3,100 as compared with $2,475 (CAW, 2012).

Adjunct Support Organizations and Strategies Used by Organizers

Although the temporary nature of adjunct employment and the previously mentioned challenges of identifying and contacting such a fluid workforce persist, specific strategies are being employed to both raise awareness of the issues surrounding "adjunctifcation" at the local and national levels and address the specific challenges of adjunct employment. Broadly speaking, strategies can be broken down into the following primary categories: (a) consciousness raising, (b) advocacy and resource sharing, and (c) organizing. Although national organizations engage in all of the categories to some degree, they do tend to specialize in one. Examples of consciousness-raising events include annual Campus Equity Week events, which began in 1999 under the leadership of COCAL and are now cosupported by New Faculty Majority, in addition to other sponsors. The purpose of Campus Equity Week events is "raising awareness and fighting to progress the issues faced by contingent educators through the United States, and partnering with activism worldwide" ("What Is Campus Equity Week," n.d.). The first National Adjunct Walkout Day took place in 2015 with a small number of actual walkouts, but it had dozens of events such as teach-ins, rallies, and talks focused on the working conditions of part-time faculty (Flaherty & Mulhere, 2015).

Perhaps the most visible development in recent years affecting part-time faculty has been an increase in advocacy, both within the academy and in society at large. A turning point that sparked both concern and action was the death of Mary Margaret Vojtko, an adjunct professor who taught for 25 years. The story of Vojtko's losing battle to retain her job in order to pay medical bills and her death from cancer was covered widely in the media and was often used by adjunct advocate organizations to highlight issues surrounding adjunct employment. National Public Radio, Slate, Huffington Post, CNN, PBS, and publications dedicated to higher education such as *The Chronicle of Higher Education* and *Inside Higher Ed* covered Vojtko's death. In response, Representative George Miller, then chair of the U.S. House Committee on Education and the Workforce, held hearings and opened an e-forum to gather information on adjunct employment. Titled *The Just-In-Time Professor*, the follow-up report highlighted the working conditions of contingent faculty in higher education and included many first-person narratives. The report further raised these issues in the public consciousness by offering an "alarming snapshot of life for contingent faculty" (House Committee on Education and the Workforce, 2014, p. 32).

One of the newer groups advocating for adjuncts is PrecariCorps. Founded in 2015, PrecariCorps provides resources regarding adjunct employment and poor working conditions, curates an archive of stories about the adjunct experience from media outlets and solicits stories from adjuncts through its blog, and supports research on adjunct faculty and their role. What makes PrecariCorps unique is its desire to address the financial plight of adjunct faculty through fund-raising and an awards program of charitable assistance and grants for living expenses or academic conference attendance (PrecariCorps, n.d.).

If one can say there is a spectrum of adjunct advocacy, with membership groups such as PrecariCorps at one end combining traditional techniques of consciousness-raising with tangible financial assistance for economically challenged adjuncts, then perhaps the other end might be represented by COCAL. Almost 20 years old, COCAL describes itself as a grassroots network of activists that supports a biennial conference and an electronic mailing list in support of organizing and advocacy activities focused on the vision of bringing "greater awareness to the precarious situation for contingent faculty in higher education, organize for action, and build solidarity among our colleagues" (COCAL International, n.d.). Though not a union, COCAL supports organizing activities and unions and hosts an electronic mailing list that aggregates a wide range of articles on adjunct organizing and provides regular updates on unionizing activities. The face of COCAL is Joe Berry, a longtime activist and academic in labor studies, who authored what many view as the handbook of adjunct organizing, *Reclaiming the Ivory Tower: Organizing Adjuncts to Change Higher Education* (Berry, 2005).

COCAL works closely with New Faculty Majority, often together supporting annual events such as Campus Equity Week. New Faculty Majority and the New Faculty Majority Foundation trace their origins back to 2009 (New Faculty Majority, n.d.-b) and have since become one of the more visible advocacy groups dedicated "to improving the quality of higher education by advancing professional equity and securing academic freedom for all adjunct and contingent faculty" (New Faculty Majority, n.d.-c). Maria Maisto, current board president of New Faculty Majority, testified before Representative George Miller's congressional hearing on November 14, 2013, on the impact of the Affordable Care Act on adjunct employment and, according to one biographical article, "has become the dominant public face of the burgeoning adjunct faculty movement" (Perloff, 2015). New Faculty Majority seeks to become the clearinghouse for information regarding adjunct advocacy and organizing and can be viewed as more research oriented as evidenced by its partnerships with the Delphi Project and the CAW, both of which function like higher education think tanks with a focus on documenting the changes in the higher education workforce and exploring and promoting potential solutions (New Faculty Majority, n.d.-c).

The most recent addition to adjunct union activities is the Service Employees International Union (SEIU). Founded in 1921, SEIU currently represents approximately two million workers in three sectors: health care (hospital, home care, and nursing home workers), public services (local and state government employees), and property services (including janitors, security officers, and food service workers) (SEIU, n.d.). SEIU has long used the strategy of organizing workers on a regional (rather than institutional) basis, having recognized that the challenge is bigger than a single institution. Building on its success in organizing adjuncts in Washington DC, and Boston, SEIU kicked off in 2014 its Adjunct Action Network (later renamed Faculty Forward) bringing its organizing skills to higher education through what has become known as the "metro organizing strategy" (Miller, 2015). Those employing this strategy "are organizing mostly faculty, and sometimes academic workers and students, into single locals that encompass not only a single campus but all campuses within a metropolitan area" (Ovetz, 2015, p. 34). By summer 2015, efforts among colleges and universities in Washington DC, had resulted in approximately 80% of adjuncts being unionized (Miller, 2015). SEIU Local 500 Executive Director David Rodick summarized the strategy: "The secret to making this work is to understand that the movement is bigger than any one individual school. No one school is broken; the system as whole is broken" (Miller, 2015, p. 49).

This "metro strategy" is being deployed by SEIU in over one dozen metro areas: by COCAL in Boston, Chicago, and New York; in Philadelphia by the American Federation of Teachers; and in the Pittsburgh region by the United Steelworkers (Berry & Worthen, 2014). Although the metro strategy is having an impact, as of 2017 it has yet to be fully implemented, and it remains to be seen if sufficient saturation of targeted metro markets will lead to the kind of solidarity envisioned by organizers. Certainly, two primary challenges face this kind of traditional union organizing among adjunct faculty. The first challenge is "to create some stability (not a feature of most contingent faculty experience) and some expectation of reliability" that could be grounded in an actual physical space, a hub where support services could be offered, a workers' center for academics (Worthen, 2015). Although this might be feasible in a limited number of metropolitan areas, the resources needed to create and sustain such an operation would be difficult to come by if dependent solely on a population with very little to spare and whose existence needs broad cooperation of many parties (Worthen, 2015). The second challenge was well summarized by Helena Worthen, a longtime union activist in higher education and retired professor who remains active in COCAL:

> The organizations that have money and could provide these resources, namely, the big teachers unions like American Federation of Teachers (AFT), American Association of University Professors, and the National Education Association, have little history of cooperation with each other. . . . Forcing the major teacher unions to collaborate on a project that costs money has happened, but on a small and usually temporary scale, not on the scale equal to the job. (Worthen, 2015, p. 424)

Although this has been the history, new levels of awareness regarding the status of adjunct faculty and the emergence of a new generation of organizers and organizations more willing to work together may overcome these traditional challenges in organizing a fluid workforce.

Remaining Challenges and Questions

Union organizing among adjunct faculty has not been without opposition, as evidenced by a protracted struggle at Northeastern University (Burns, 2013) and issues raised over the opposition to unions at Catholic-affiliated universities, whose values traditionally supported the freedom of labor to organize (Schmidt, 2013). Faculty themselves are often divided, as full-time faculty sometimes resist organizing efforts on the part of adjuncts, believing that such efforts may erode their own power within the institution (Schmidt, 2014). Among union organizers themselves, the immediate and long-term goals are often not agreed on. Some advocate for more tenure-track positions, and others focus on improving working conditions for adjunct faculty, though these emphases are not mutually exclusive. Adrianna Kezar, cofounder of the Delphi Project, whose research focuses on how the changing faculty affects student success, has suggested a middle ground. Kezar recommended that adjunct advocates and organizers begin to promote alternative hiring models, believing that longer term salaried contracts with benefits can address the challenges faced by both faculty and administrators: "Many administrators cannot see an alternative that is viable for institutions in financial difficulties, especially in the context of no public support for higher education" (Segran, 2014). Kezar is among an increasing number of advocates and researchers who call for universities to do more to assist adjunct and all non-tenure-track faculty by providing more professional development opportunities (Segran, 2014). Thus, the questions that have guided our research are twofold: What is the current status of adjunct faculty development, and what are the best practices that may be used to support adjunct faculty? Our findings constitute the remainder of this book.

References

Abrams, M. (2006, Spring). ASJMC adjunct survey results . . . and more. *ASJMC Insights, 2006,* 18–22. Retrieved from http://www.asjmc.org/publications/insights/spring2006.pdf

AFT Higher Education. (2010). *American academic: A national survey of part-time adjunct faculty.* Washington, DC: Author. Retrieved from http://www.aft.org/sites/default/files/aa_partimefaculty0310.pdf

Allison, M., Lynn, R., & Hoverman, V. (2014, October). *Indispensable but invisible: A report on the working climate of non-tenure track faculty at George Mason University.* Fairfax, VA: Public Sociology Association, George Mason University. Retrieved from https://contingentfacultystudy.files.wordpress.com/2013/08/gmu-contingent-faculty-study.pdf

American Association of University Professors. (2016). *Higher education at a crossroads: The annual report on the economic status of the profession, 2015–16.* Washington, DC: Author. Retrieved from https://www.aaup.org/report/higher-education-crossroads-annual-report-economic-status-profession-2015-16

Anderson, L. V. (2013, November 17). Death of a professor. *Slate.* Retrieved from http://www.slate.com/articles/news_and_politics/education/2013/11/death_of_duquesne_adjunct_margaret_mary_vojtko_what_really_happened_to_her.html

Antony, J. S., & Valadez, J. R. (2002). Exploring the satisfaction of part-time college faculty in the United States. *The Review of Higher Education, 26*(1), 41–56. doi:10.1353/rhe.2002.0023

Austin, A. E., & Gamson, Z. F. (1983). *Academic workplace: New demands, heightened tensions* (ASHE-ERIC Higher Education Report, No. 10). Washington, DC: Association for the Study of Higher Education. Retrieved from http://eric.ed.gov/?id=ED243397

Belkin, D., & Korn, M. (2015, February 16). Colleges' use of adjuncts comes under pressure. *The Wall Street Journal.* Retrieved from http://www.wsj.com/articles/colleges-use-of-adjunct-instructors-comes-under-pressure-1424118108

Berry, J. (2005). *Reclaiming the ivory tower: Organizing adjuncts to change higher education.* New York, NY: Monthly Review Press.

Berry, J., & Savaris, M. (2012). *Directory of U.S. faculty contracts and bargaining agents in institutions of higher education.* New York, NY: The National Center for the Study of Collective Bargaining in Higher Education and the Professions.

Berry, J., & Worthen, H. (2014, October 9). 22 states where adjunct faculty are organizing for justice. *In These Times.* Retrieved from http://inthesetimes.com/working/entry/17233/wave_of_contingent_faculty_organizing_sweeps_onto_campuses

Bureau of Labor Statistics. (2016, January 28). Union members summary [News release]. Retrieved from http://www.bls.gov/news.release/union2.nr0.htm

Burns, R. (2013, August 29). University tries to nip professors' union in the bud. *In These Times.* Retrieved from http://inthesetimes.com/article/15531/northeastern_tries_to_quelch_adjnuct_unin

Coalition on the Academic Workforce. (2012). *A portrait of part-time faculty members: A summary of findings on part-time faculty respondents to the Coalition on the Academic Workforce survey of contingent faculty members and instructors.* Retrieved from http://www.academicworkforce.org/CAW_portrait_2012.pdf

COCAL International. (n.d.). About us. Retrieved from http://cocalinternational.org/

Cross, J. G., & Goldenberg, E. N. (2009). *Off-track profs: Non-tenured teachers in higher education.* Cambridge, MA: MIT Press.

DeCew, J. (2003). *Unionization in the academy*. Lanham, MD: Rowman & Littlefield.

The disposable academic: Why doing a PhD is often a waste of time. (2010, December 16). *The Economist*. Retrieved from http://www.economist.com/node/17723223?story_id=17723223

Dougherty, K., Rhoades, G., & Smith, M. (2014). Bargaining for part-time contingent faculty. *The NEA Almanac of Higher Education, 2014, 53*–64. Retrieved from http://www.nea.org/assets/docs/HE/2014_Almanac_DoughertyRhoades-Smith.pdf

Dunn, S. (2014, August 1). Where in the world are the adjunct unions? Vitae. Retrieved from https://chroniclevitae.com/news/639-where-in-the-world-are-the-adjunct-unions

Eagan, M. K., Jaeger, A. J., & Grantham, A. (2015). Supporting the academic majority: Policies and practices related to part-time faculty's job satisfaction. *Journal of Higher Education, 86*(3), 448–483. doi:10.1353/jhe.2015.0012

Feldman, D. C., & Turnley, W. H. (2001). A field study of adjunct faculty: The impact of career stage on reactions to non-tenure-track jobs. *Journal of Career Development, 28*, 1–16. doi:10.1177/089484530102800101

Flaherty, C., & Mulhere, K. (2015, February 26). Day of protest. *Inside Higher Ed*. Retrieved from https://www.insidehighered.com/news/2015/02/26/adjuncts-deem-national-walkout-day-success

Gappa, J. (2000). The new faculty majority: Somewhat satisfied but not eligible for tenure. *New Directions for Institutional Research, 2000*(105), 77–86. doi:10.1002/ir.10507

Gappa, J. M., & Leslie, D. W. (1993). *The invisible faculty: Improving the status of part-timers in higher education*. San Francisco, CA: Jossey-Bass.

Hightower, J. (2014). The symbolism of one adjunct professor's death [Blog post]. Retrieved from http://www.jimhightower.com/node/8283#.VN4mhfnF98E

House Committee on Education and the Workforce. (2014). *The just-in-time professor: A staff report summarizing eforum responses on the working conditions of contingent faculty in higher education*. Washington, DC: Author. Retrieved from http://democrats.edworkforce.house.gov/sites/democrats.edworkforce.house.gov/files/documents/1.24.14-AdjunctEforumReport.pdf

Is academia suffering from "adjunctivitis"? Low-paid adjunct professors struggle to make ends meet [Video file]. (2014, February 6). *PBS Newshour*. Retrieved from http://www.pbs.org/newshour/bb/is-academia-suffering-adjunctivitis/

Jacobs, K., Perry, I., & MacGillvary, J. (2015). The high public cost of low wages: Poverty-level wages cost U.S. taxpayers $152.8 billion each year in public support for working families [Research brief]. Retrieved from http://laborcenter.berkeley.edu/pdf/2015/the-high-public-cost-of-low-wages.pdf

Jacoby, D. (2005). Part-time community-college faculty and the desire for full-time tenure-track positions: Results of a single institution case study. *Community College Journal of Research and Practice, 29*, 137–152.

Jaeger, A. J. (2008). Contingent faculty and student outcomes. *Academe, 94*(6), 42–43. Retrieved from http://www.jstor.org/stable/40253276

Johnson, K. (2015). *Ideologies, typologies, and inequalities: Efforts to understand adjunct faculty.* Manuscript submitted for publication.

Kezar, A., & Gehrke, S. (2013). Creating a high-quality place to teach, learn, and work. *Peer Review, 15*(3). Retrieved from https://www.aacu.org/peerreview/2013/summer/kezar-gehrke

Kezar, A., & Holcombe, E. (2015). The professoriate reconsidered: What might the faculty look like in 2050? *Academe, 101*(6). Retrieved from http://www.aaup.org/article/professoriate-reconsidered#.VyJWA6grKUl

Kezar, A., & Maxey, D. (2012). Missing from the institutional data picture: Non-tenure-track faculty. *New Directions for Institutional Research, 2012*(155), 47–65. doi:10.1002/ir.20021

Kezar, A., & Maxey, D. (2014). Troubling ethical lapses: The treatment of contingent faculty. *Change, 46*(4), 34–37. doi:10.1080/00091383.2014.925761

Kramer, A. L., Gloeckner, G. W., & Jacoby, D. (2014). Roads scholars: Part-time faculty job satisfaction in community colleges. *Community College Journal of Research and Practice, 38*(4), 287–299.

Leslie, D. W., & Gappa, J. M. (1997). Education's new academic work force. In G. Keller (Ed.), *The best of planning for higher education: An anthology of articles from the premier journal in higher education planning* (pp. 61–66). Ann Arbor, MI: Society for College and University Planning.

Leslie, D. W., & Gappa, J. M. (2002). Part-time faculty: Competent and committed. *New Directions for Community Colleges, 2002*(118). doi:10.1002/cc.64

Maynard, D., & Joseph, T. (2008). Are all part-time faculty underemployed? The influence of faculty status preference on satisfaction and commitment. *Higher Education, 55*(2), 139–154. doi:10.1007/s10734-006-9039-z

Miller, J. (2015, June 30). When adjuncts go union. *The American Prospect.* Retrieved from http://prospect.org/article/when-adjuncts-go-union

Muncaster, K. (2011). *Supporting adjunct faculty within the academy: From road scholars to retired sages, one size does not fit all* (Doctoral dissertation). Retrieved from http://hdl.handle.net/2345/2426

National Center for Education Statistics. (2015). Characteristics of postsecondary faculty. Retrieved from http://nces.ed.gov/programs/coe/indicator_cuf.asp

New Faculty Majority. (n.d.-a). Are adjuncts organizing in the U.S.? Retrieved from http://www.newfacultymajority.info/faqs-frequently-asked-questions/are-adjuncts-organizing-in-the-u-s/

New Faculty Majority. (n.d.-b). History. Retrieved from http://www.newfacultymajority.info/history-and-foundational-principles/

New Faculty Majority. (n.d.-c). NFM mission. Retrieved from http://www.newfacultymajority.info/nfm-mission-statement/

O'Meara, K., LaPointe Terosky, A., & Neumann, A. (2008). Faculty careers and work lives: A professional growth perspective. *ASHE Higher Education Report, 34*(3), 1–221.

Ovetz, R. (2015). Migrant mindworkers and the new division of academic labor. *Working USA: The Journal of Labor and Society, 18*, 331–347. doi:10.1111/wusa.12184

Perloff, R. (2015, July 7). From comp lit to the adjunct's champion: The academic odyssey of Maria Maisto. *Belt Magazine*. Retrieved from http://beltmag.com/from-comp-lit-to-the-adjuncts-champion-the-academic-odyssey-of-maria-maisto/

PrecariCorps. (n.d.). Programs. Retrieved from https://precaricorps.org/programs/

Rhoades, G. (2012). Bargaining quality in part-time faculty working conditions: Beyond just-in-time employment and just-at-will non-renewal. *Journal of Collective Bargaining in the Academy, 4*. Retrieved from http://thekeep.eiu.edu/jcba/vol4/iss1/4

Rhoades, G. (2015). Creative leveraging in contingent faculty organizing. *Working USA: The Journal of Labor and Society, 18*, 435–445. doi:10.1111/wusa.12191

Rosvosky, H. (1980). *The university: An owner's manual*. New York, NY: W. W. Norton.

Schmidt, P. (2013, December 9). Adjuncts appeal to higher power in debate over unions at religious colleges. *The Chronicle of Higher Education*. Retrieved from http://chronicle.com/article/Debates-Over-Religious/143493/

Schmidt, P. (2014, April 9). Union efforts on behalf of adjuncts meet resistance within faculties' ranks. *The Chronicle of Higher Education*. Retrieved from http://chronicle.com/article/Union-Efforts-on-Behalf-of/145833

Schmidt, P. (2015, March 9). Adjunct advocacy: Contingent faculty members are demanding—and getting—better working conditions. *The Chronicle of Higher Education*. Retrieved from http://chronicle.com/article/Adjunct-advocacy-Contingent/228155

Schuster, J. H., & Finkelstein, M. J. (2006). *The American faculty: The restructuring of academic work and careers*. Baltimore, MD: John Hopkins University Press.

Schwartz, J. (2007). Professional development geared to part-timers' needs: An adjunct professor's perspective. In R. E. Lyons (Ed.), *Best practices for supporting adjunct faculty* (pp. 241–251). Boston, MA: Anker.

Segran, E. (2014, April 28). The adjunct revolt: How poor professors are fighting back. *The Atlantic*. Retrieved from http://www.theatlantic.com/business/archive/2014/04/the-adjunct-professor-crisis/361336/

Service Employees International Union. (n.d.). What type of work do SEIU members do? Retrieved from http://www.seiu.org/cards/these-fast-facts-will-tell-you-how-were-organized/what-type-of-work-do-seiu-members-do/p1

Smith, R. (2015, September 1). The social injustice done to adjunct faculty: A call to arms. *Public Discourse*. Retrieved from http://www.thepublicdiscourse.com/2015/09/14452/

Spector, H. (2013). Part-time college faculty fight for better pay and working conditions. *The Plain Dealer*. Retrieved from http://www.cleveland.com/metro/index.ssf/2013/05/part-time_faculty_organize_to.html

Street, S., Maisto, M., Merves, E., & Rhoades, G. (2012, August). Who is Professor "Staff": And how can this person teach so many classes? *Inside Higher Ed*. Retrieved from https://www.insidehighered.com/sites/default/server_files/files/profstaff(2).pdf

Toutkoushian, R., & Bellas, M. (2003). The effects of part-time employment and gender on faculty earnings and satisfaction: Evidence from the NSOPF:93. *Journal of Higher Education, 74*, 172–195.

Townsend, R. B., & Hauss, M. E. (2002, October). The 2002 AHA-OAH survey of part-time and adjunct faculty. *Perspectives on History.* Retrieved from https://www.historians.org/publications-and-directories/perspectives-on-history/october-2002/the-2002-aha-oah-survey-of-part-time-and-adjunct-faculty

Tuckman, H. P. (1978). Who is part-time in academe? *Bulletin of the American Association of University Professors, 64*, 305–315. doi:10.2307/40225146

Umbach, P. D. (2007). How effective are they? Exploring the impact of contingent faculty on undergraduate education. *The Review of Higher Education, 30*, 91–123. doi:10.1353/rhe.2006.0080

What is Campus Equity Week? (n.d.). Retrieved from http://www.campusequityweek.org/2013/about-2/

Worthen, H. (2015). Organizing as learning: The metro strategy and a community of practice for faculty. *Working USA: The Journal of Labor and Society, 18*, 421–433. doi:10.1111/wusa.12190

2

Adjunct Voices

Roy Fuller

The unique stories of adjunct faculty are often not heard or prominently featured in national conversations about adjunct faculty in higher education. Our goal with *Adjunct Faculty Voices: Cultivating Professional Development and Community at the Front Lines of Higher Education* is multifaceted. First, we want to provide an overview of the demographics of adjunct faculty and current best practices in providing professional development opportunities for this growing segment of the academic workforce. Second, we want to tell the stories of adjunct faculty who have sought and sometimes found community and professional development opportunities. Knowledge of both areas is important for administrators seeking to support adjunct faculty who are teaching a majority of courses on many campuses.

As we began our work on this project, we developed a call for proposals to invite submissions from adjunct faculty across the country and across the disciplines regarding their experiences with professional development opportunities and other types of institutional support for teaching and their success in finding and creating communities of practice. We also sought submissions that would offer advice to other adjuncts seeking professional development opportunities related to teaching improvement and recommendations for deans, department chairs, course coordinators, and/or faculty developers for improving support structures for adjunct faculty.

The call was promoted through professional electronic mailing lists and social media for adjunct faculty and educational developers. We sought participants' help in distributing our call to other adjunct faculty with whom they are in contact. We received over 30 submissions that touched on one or more of the areas noted in the call. We evaluated how well the submissions addressed the call themes and the overall quality, how the submissions supported their claims by connecting to appropriate literature, and the degree to which the submissions supported the broad purposes of the work as a whole. We selected a total of nine for inclusion in this book. To richly represent the adjunct experience, we included diverse perspectives with respect to the type of story told. For example, many adjunct faculty may fall into more than one of the traditional categories of adjunct faculty as articulated by Gappa and Leslie (1993), may simultaneously represent more than one, and may follow a career arc from "aspiring" to "retiring." For this reason, we chose to organize these selections in terms of the type of relationship each writer articulated to oneself, one's colleagues, and one's institution or institutions, as some adjunct faculty teach at multiple institutions.

As adjunct faculty often work in isolation, with little to no contact with other faculty and administrators, we begin with selections about evaluating personal and professional strengths as educators. Brandon Hensley describes the power of personal narrative in making connections to his experiences of inclusion and exclusion within academia. Personifying this approach, Victoria Shropshire details her own professional development path and describes how such opportunities can enhance one's teaching and open the doors to a more fulfilling career in academia.

A significant issue facing adjunct faculty is that of lack of community. The next set of submissions is therefore connected by themes of community and how it can be created by adjuncts themselves. Chris Potts traces his journey from longing for community to his own initial effort to create community and the hesitant institutional responses he received. Paul G. Putman and Bridget A. Kriner offer a *communities of practice* model that evolved into an ongoing support network that continues to provide opportunities for feedback on research, employment searches, and teaching practice for the participants.

These writers share their personal stories, opportunities found and not found for community and inclusion, and considerations for how adjunct faculty interact with the institutions that employ them. As such, these selections offer opportunities for other adjunct faculty and administrators to gain insight into the adjunct experience and empower them to explore ways their own institutions can promote and support adjunct faculty. When faculty are supported in their teaching through having access to professional development opportunities, opportunities for community with colleagues, and recognition for their work, student learning is improved, a goal just about everyone in higher education believes is worth striving toward.

Reference

Gappa, J. M., & Leslie, D. W. (1993). *The invisible faculty: Improving the status of part-timers in higher education*. San Francisco, CA: Jossey-Bass.

3

Cocreating Communities of Adjunct Faculty

Mobilizing Adjunct Voices Through Connective Storytelling

Brandon Hensley

The academic profession has slowly but inexorably become bifurcated into two faculties: the tenured "haves" and the temporary, part-time "have-nots."... The low costs and heavy undergraduate teaching loads of the have-nots make possible the continuation of a tenure system that protects the jobs and perquisites of the haves.

—Gappa and Leslie (1993, p. 2)

The story I *want* to tell is one of faculty uniting as a plurivocal community of scholars, learners, and teachers in the interest of student learning and fair treatment for all who teach (and all who are aspiring to teach). Instead, the only storyline echoing in my head is one that troubles me every day—of the inequity, systematic divisions (between tenure-line faculty and adjuncts), and obstacles that adjunct faculty face in twenty-first-century American higher education (Hensley, 2016).

I yearn for an alternative narrative that calls attention to the importance of sharing adjunct stories, in both scholarly and viral (social media) forms. If educators in academe ever wish to have an inclusive community of scholars and teachers, bridging the gaps of misunderstanding and misrepresentation (or addressing the problem of no representation) is a start to inviting room for hope in the future of postsecondary education and adjunct working conditions.

In this chapter, I forward the argument that adjuncts writing and circulating personal narratives can make significant headway in connecting disparate factions of college personnel, whether they be adjunct, tenure line, multiyear contracted, graduate teaching assistants, administrators, or trustees. The gap or disconnect among faculty, felt most brutally by adjuncts, is multifaceted: a lack of tenured–adjunct faculty interaction; narrow conceptions held by tenured faculty and administration of adjunct faculty as a generalized group; and subtle and overt forms of discrimination and oppression in issues of pay equity, governance, and other aspects of adjuncts' subordinate employment conditions. This chapter is a tentative attempt to envision how adjunct storytelling might cultivate narratives that foster a sense of community among faculty, as well as with administrators and others in positions of power who can advocate for better adjunct faculty working conditions. I use my personal experience as an adjunct professor and draw on the research–writing method of autoethnography as a vehicle to connect adjunct voices and disseminate their struggle to audiences inside and outside the academy. *Autoethnography* is generally defined as the use of personal narrative in analyzing and critiquing culture (Holman Jones, Adams, & Ellis, 2013; see also Boylorn & Orbe, 2014; C. Ellis, 2004; Goodall, 2000).

I will briefly story my lived experience of paradoxical inclusion and exclusion as an adjunct: inclusion into teaching diverse courses and serving in various volunteer service positions at the institution where I teach but being totally excluded from faculty governance and professional development, reward, and promotion channels. I will trace a significant viral story of adjunct maltreatment and call for more critical stories (via autoethnographies or other evocative writing forms that rely on personal narrative) to fracture dominant narratives of postsecondary faculty in the United States and bring about social justice in the treatment of adjuncts across American higher education.

My Story

I've worked as an adjunct at a small, private, nonprofit university for five years now. In 2010, when I was in the last semester of my master's degree program (where I was a graduate teaching assistant [TA]) at a midsize, midwestern state university, one of my teachers told me he knew a department chair at a nearby school looking for people to teach Public Speaking. He "hinted" I should send my curriculum vitae along to the chair and copy him in the e-mail. The only familiarity I had with the school he mentioned was its name.

I remember feeling unbridled excitement when I got an e-mail from the chair asking me to visit campus to talk about a job position. It seemed too good to be true: I had a shot of getting a college teaching job right out of my master's program, the prospective university wasn't too far, and it was small and private. I didn't know how small or how private. For me, "small and private" would come to mean implicit and explicit exclusion, as an adjunct, from the select (read: full-time, tenure-track, and tenured) community of faculty who could serve on the faculty senate, apply for teaching research awards, receive insurance coverage and benefits, and so on. Looking back now, as I am finishing my dissertation—a qualitative exploration of adjunct faculty dichotomization and dehumanization in U.S. higher education—I realize how inaccurate and "rose colored" my initial perceptions were.

My first day at Chimera University (pseudonym) took me from the relatively drab, hodge-podge architecture campus I'd been at for six years completing my bachelor's and master's degrees—picture a gleaming glass Business Hall adjacent to a 1960s brutalist architecture building where the arts and humanities classes and my TA office were housed—to a small, tree-lined campus with uniform Elizabethan red-brick buildings, exquisitely manicured grounds, and a population of about 2,300 students who were paying approximately $30,000 a year in tuition alone to be there. As a point of comparison, students at the school I attended for my degrees paid roughly half that (including housing, dining, and fees).

This was my first encounter with a campus that fit the archetype of what some still think of when they hear "college." If one judges "college" to be an amalgamation of media representations of grassy quadrangles, clock towers, ornate buildings with columns, and tweed-clad, frazzled professors walking to class with an aloof yet hip demeanor, this was it.

The interview for my adjunct position was more like a 15-minute talk about what days and times I'd like to teach Public Speaking (because I'd be commuting for the first semester) and what other courses I'd be interested in teaching for the department. I was flabbergasted by the ease of the interview; this wasn't what I'd observed in graduate school when a job candidate would come in for interviewing. It was usually a multiday interview with lots of meet and greets, research presentations, and sample teaching lessons, all of which I was ready to deliver. Instead, I was given paperwork and, within one week, keys to the adjunct office and a parking pass. Reflecting back now, I think, *It was too good to be true. Chimerical, but at the time it seemed like a dream come true.*

At this predominantly baccalaureate-granting institution, the department was small—three tenured faculty (one of whom was the chair) and five adjunct faculty. The summer before my teaching appointment began, images of faculty collegiality permeated my view of Chimera University, partly because of the intimate, picturesque campus and impressive brick-and-mortar feel of the institution and partly because the few people I met seemed nice and welcoming. Immediately, I thought, *Wow, faculty must love teaching at this beautiful school! With such a lovely campus, it must be a tight-knit community.* Never mind that I wasn't invited to the faculty orientation week (only full-time faculty are contacted and expected to take part) and I didn't really know anybody except for the chair, administrative assistant, and staff in human resources. The first semester was, in a way, like trying to navigate an impressive sea vessel, only to realize there are a lot of unexpected surprises, problems, and feelings of isolation.

In the short time I've been teaching at Chimera University, I've taught as many as four courses per semester and as few as two. These have ranged from the basic Public Speaking course to upper-level courses in media effects, crisis communication, research methods, interpersonal communication, and intercultural communication. While teaching, I've pursued a PhD in higher education administration and foundations at a nearby public university and completed all course work and qualifying exams, and I'm currently in the dissertation phase. Because my aspiration is to continue teaching at the university level—eventually with a full-time or tenure-track position—I fall into the category of "hopeful full-timer" (Tuckman, 1978, p. 308) or "aspiring academic" (Gappa & Leslie, 1993).

The first semesters at Chimera afforded me many opportunities to teach different courses, so I was initially blinded to the meager pay I was receiving and the adjunct-induced barriers I faced when attempting to be a contributing member of the campus community. I was very much involved on campus with advising student organizations but was on the outside looking in when it came to being treated like a valued faculty member. For example, in spring 2011, I was invited by students to be faculty editor for a campus multiculturalism newsletter called *Diversity Talk*. A year later, I was asked by administration in residence life to serve as a faculty sponsor for an academic-focused living learning community. Most recently, after being approached by the student body president and dean of students, I accepted an invitation to Student Senate as the faculty advocate, a liaison between the student body and full-time faculty. All of this, in addition to writing letters of recommendation, doing assessment work, and showing support at students' athletics and arts events, was and is campus involvement I find to be very fulfilling.

However, when I try to perform my role as an engaged member of the faculty—attempting to serve on faculty committees, applying for the Teaching Excellence award, trying to secure grant funding (available to full-time faculty) for my work on the assessment coordinator report only to be told by an administrator, "There's no money, we can have someone else do it if you don't want to"—I find myself feeling devalued and shut off from matters of faculty governance, recognition, and representation. When I try to be a member of the (exclusive, tenure-track) faculty community, I hit a red-brick wall. I'm lucky I shared an adjunct office with three other adjuncts who could commiserate with me about our struggles. That was the closest sense of community (outside of the sense of community forged with my students) that I experienced at Chimera University, both when I first started and now that I'm going into my sixth year.

Connecting to the Stories of Others

I'll never forget where I was when I read of the death (and life) of Margaret Mary Vojtko. I was sitting on the couch in my apartment in Decatur, Georgia, checking my multiple e-mail accounts: school where I teach, school where I am a student, Yahoo, Gmail where I direct various correspondence (I think I'm up to seven now). An e-mail from an old teacher and friend caught my eye: *For Your Adjunct Project.* Attached was a link to an article in *The Chronicle of Higher Education* with the headline "An Adjunct's Death Becomes a Rallying Cry for Many in Academe." I read that the university where this adjunct had worked for 25 years "reduced [professor] Vojtko's course load to one class per semester last fall, decreasing her annual earnings to below $10,000. Ms. Vojtko, a cancer patient, could not afford electricity in her home" (Ellis, 2013, para. 5).

I called my grandma soon after reading the news of Vojtko's death, not to talk about the story but to connect with her. We have talked on the phone at least once a week ever since I first went to college as a freshman; these calls have been part of the relational maintenance of our close grandparent–grandchild bond. I didn't call her to tell her about a shocking piece I had read by Daniel Kovalik (2013) in which he wrote as a colleague in lucid first-person about possibly being the last person to talk to Margaret Mary. He described the last phone call between the two:

> She told me that she was under an incredible amount of stress. She was receiving radiation therapy for the cancer that had just returned to her, she was living nearly homeless because she could not afford the upkeep on her home, which was literally falling in on itself, and now . . . a letter from Adult Protective Services telling her that . . . she needed assistance in taking care of herself. (para. 2)

I did not tell my grandma about this because I didn't want her to worry. She thinks I will be full-time and/or president of a university soon. I don't want her to worry that I fear I'll never move "up" from a job that pays around $15,000 a year with no insurance and no guarantees of being promoted, offered a yearly contract, or rehired. I don't want to tell her that my university teaching experience isn't like what she thinks of when she hears "college professor."

My grandma is 92 years old and has no doubt lived a full life, largely because of remaining mentally active and living moderately as well as because of the excellent health care she has received (from my grandpa's insurance as a state employee). She and my grandpa took numerous trips to the Mayo Clinic when I was a kid, and whenever a health issue came up, there was never any worry that they wouldn't be covered. In the past year, my grandpa passed on, but he left my grandma a comfortable pension, life insurance plan, and account at Edward Jones.

I wonder what life would have been like if their employments were so brutal to them that they didn't have pensions, first-rate health insurance, life insurance, and so on. Grandma has told me many times that she is living through me, because she always wanted to be a college teacher. I wondered, What if it were *my* grandma who worked herself to death as an adjunct professor? What if *I* work myself to death as an adjunct?

The Power of Stories to Create Change

Adjunct stories need to be heard. The horrible treatment experienced by Margaret Mary Vojtko and other adjunct faculty in the United States needs to continue to be written about, shared, circulated, and promoted. It is through stories of struggle that community can emerge, first among fellow contingent faculty, and then ripple through faculty ranks, administration, and external publics. To create community, there needs to be understanding, and what way is more practical than telling a true story, not in academese but in language that is accessible and provocative?

The adjunct social movement has arguably already begun with the death of Margaret Mary Vojtko. From here, stories that evocatively capture the lived experiences of contingent faculty can add to the flame that has been lit in a dark corner of academia. If students are to succeed in a globally competitive environment that demands skill sets of critical thinking, intercultural competence, and writing and communication skills (among myriad specialized skills), how can institutions continue to treat the majority of the faculty body as second-class academics, at-will employees, and exploited educators?

Listening to the stories of adjunct faculty reveals that the answer is clear: For many adjuncts, the working conditions are brutal and position them in a lower tier than full-time and tenured and tenure-track faculty. The current pervasive maltreatment of contingent faculty is not sustainable for institutions or those who labor under these conditions, and adjuncts' stories help expose this dichotomization and dehumanization to the American public (e.g., parents of prospective students, alumni, current and future students, etc.). To paraphrase Tim O'Brien (1990) in *The Things They Carried*, this too is true: Stories can save us. Stories can help galvanize us as faculty members and people who deserve to be treated equitably, and stories can turn the tide of adjunct faculty subordination. Margaret Mary Vojtko's story, among other stories I've read and heard, needs to reach more people all over the United States, from prospective students and families to power brokers in the ivory tower. The push for change has begun, but there is much work, storytelling, and critical reflection yet to be done.

References

Boylorn, R. M., & Orbe, M. P. (Eds.). (2014). *Critical autoethnography: Intersecting cultural identities in everyday life*. Walnut Creek, CA: Left Coast Press.

Ellis, C. (2004). *The ethnographic I: A methodological novel about autoethnography*. Walnut Creek, CA: AltaMira Press.

Ellis, L. (2013, September 19). An adjunct's death becomes a rallying cry for many in academe. *The Chronicle of Higher Education*. Retrieved from http://chronicle.com/article/An-Adjuncts-Death-Becomes-a/141709/

Gappa, J. M., & Leslie, D. W. (1993). *The invisible faculty: Improving the status of part-timers in higher education*. San Francisco, CA: Jossey-Bass.

Goodall, H. L. (2000). *Writing the new ethnography*. Walnut Creek, CA: AltaMira Press.

Hensley, B. O. (2016). *Adjunct faculty in a neoliberal age: The power of critical stories* (Unpublished doctoral dissertation). Illinois State University, Normal, IL.

Holman Jones, S., Adams, T. E., & Ellis, C. (Eds.). (2013). *Handbook of autoethnography*. Walnut Creek, CA: Left Coast Press.

Kovalik, D. (2013, September 18). Underpaid 83-year-old professor died trying to make ends meet by working night shift at Eat an' Save. *AlterNet*. Retrieved from http://www.alternet.org/economy/underpaid-83-year-old-professor-died-trying-make-ends-meet-working-night-shift-eat-save

O'Brien, T. (1990). *The things they carried*. Boston, MA: Houghton Mifflin.

Tuckman, H. P. (1978). Who is part-time in academe? *AAUP Bulletin, 64*(4), 305–315. doi:10.2307/40225146

4

Exiting the Freeway Faculty Path

Using Professional Development to Get Out of Cruise Control

Victoria Shropshire

*F*reeway faculty* have a unique opportunity to engage with multiple learners in a variety of academic settings, and professional development opportunities can make them not only superior instructors who respond to our changing society and its students but also be the "exit" they need to pursue other career possibilities.

The Development of a Professional

I would consider myself a hybrid of two adjunct genres (Gappa & Leslie, 1993) as a *freelancer* and a *specialist*, although I am currently pursuing my doctorate, which I suppose officially makes me an *aspiring academic*. Because of my degrees in English and writing and years of professional writing experience, combined with the ever-increasing hiring of adjuncts to teach in the core university disciplines (Miller, 2014), I have never had any problems finding adjunct or limited-term contract work on a college campus. I currently teach at a small private four-year liberal arts university in the South, which has provided me with multiple supportive and structured professional development systems, all available to *any* university faculty member. It is painfully clear to me that adjuncts need professional development opportunities as much as colleges and universities need adjuncts for teaching.

> In today's world, and in the foreseeable future, teachers will need to engage in high-quality professional development if they are to keep pace with and respond to changes in society and, at the same time, retain their energy, enthusiasm, and commitment to high-quality teaching. (Day & Sachs, 2005, p. 14)

46

Because freeway faculty engage with multiple learners in a variety of academic settings and institutions, they may have access to more professional development opportunities than they realize. Although it is often challenging for an adjunct instructor to budget the time for them, they are worth every moment. Professional development and access to mentors can not only make you a superior instructor but also open new roads for you to pursue other career paths.

Freeway Faculty

While I was an adjunct instructor for a total of 10 years, from 1998 to 2000 and 2005 to 2011, I was affectionately labeled what we in the South call *freeway faculty*, a term used to describe college adjunct instructors who (like me) managed multiple teaching gigs, simultaneously teaching any combination of hybrids, online, and face-to-face (F-2-F) courses for multiple community colleges and/or four-year universities through substantial mileage on the highways. (At one point, while living in the Smoky Mountains, I put 100 miles on my car every day that I taught on two different college campuses.) There were frustrating moments, when the ridiculous pay and the amount of cash I poured into my gas tank made me want to toss it all in and become a barista at Starbucks, where, I reasoned, at least they got health care. But I didn't. I had held extremely lucrative jobs prior to becoming a full-time educator, but they were unfulfilling. Working in the entertainment industry had drained me, and working in advertising had been soul sucking; only in education did I find the perfect fit for my talents, energy, and creativity. And so I, like virtually every other adjunct colleague I know, chose a life one step from abject poverty because I believe in my students, I have a passion for my job, I have an interest in the success of our students, and I have a desire to personally and professionally improve every semester, rather than crank out the same curriculum, regardless of whether it is engaging or impactful. Although full-time positions are increasingly rare in the world of academia, adjunct positions abound.

Adjunct instruction, for a variety of reasons, is the only choice in some academic regions, even though some choose it deliberately. Nearly "75 percent of the teaching faculty on college campuses is done by adjuncts" (Miller, 2014, p. 25). After moving from Texas to the Smoky Mountains of North Carolina, I found that the freeway faculty life was my only option to keep doing what I love. Later, moving to the Piedmont region of the same state, I chose to stay an adjunct not only for the freedom it provided me but also because I discovered that being in constant motion lends itself to a very palpable forward momentum that comprises all adjunct lives, freeway or not. Find these souls and form a sort of casual support group, even if it's just to meet on Thursday mornings for coffee. The truth is that when you are an adjunct, no one will ever understand you better. Look across the disciplines and ask those in staffed departments that may be available on your campus, such as Center for the Advancement of Teaching and Learning (CATL), Scholarship of Teaching and Learning (SoTL), or Teaching and Learning Technologies (TLT), who are often best positioned to help you find other adjuncts. These individuals are everywhere and are probably looking for someone just like you, too. The adjunct heart is great, and the numbers of adjuncts keeping America's universities running tells you that teaching for the sake of teaching has a powerful heartbeat as well.

Risk It

Successful adjuncts, in my experience, are those willing to try new things, to learn new techniques, to hone new skills, and to take risks. I have often believed that they are eager to attend seminars and workshops that highlight new teaching tools and strategies. I find that freeway faculty have a flexible skill set that tenured folks either never had or have forgotten; the view is much changed between the campus window and the windshield. Not having to worry about promotion and tenure politics, requisite commitments of committee work, or other "cruise control" administrative trappings can be capitalized on in the life of the freeway faculty. Adjuncts come from a wide range of backgrounds and fields of expertise, and many are able to integrate these real-world experiences into their academic lessons and environment. So if a university is looking for unique insight or innovation in the classroom to assist in the marriage of education and experience, adjuncts should be first in line. It may seem like you simply don't have the time to invest in new tools or strategies, but in my experience, you will find the time if you make this a higher priority. Don't delete those professional development e-mails that are sent en masse to the entire faculty. In attending these seminars and workshops, you will not only gain new skills and ideas but also often find assistance and camaraderie among other adjunct instructors who are, like you, interested in creative and innovative techniques that engage students and increase learning. Quality professional development supercharges the engines of effective instructors who are freeway faculty.

Flex It

I discovered that adjuncts who teach at multiple colleges simultaneously, as I did, had the opportunity to try a classroom exercise or writing prompt on a variety of learners with a wide range of learning styles and often adapted quickly to improve in multiple arenas with multiple approaches to the same series of learning outcomes. For example, once I learned, through one-on-one professional development, how to improve my course design using a learning management system (LMS), my entire teaching career changed instantly and immeasurably. Students interacted more directly with difficult course material, actually reading prior to class meetings (gasp), which greatly improved the quality of discourse during those classes, as well as increased the critical thinking they applied to their reading and writing. They engaged with the ideas and then wrote better papers, I suffered fewer headaches, and they earned higher grades. Win, win, win.

This flexibility and willingness to try new things became my own entry into organized professional learning because I instantly saw benefits in student engagement, learning, and assessment. I was doing more for them with less stress, they were getting more from my class and making more of an effort, and we were all loving it. By *organized* professional development, I mean structured, established, often sponsored and funded professional development opportunities, from small campus reading groups to large-scale conferences. Prior to being contacted by someone at my teaching center, my only form of professional development was learning the basics of Blackboard at a colleague's kitchen table.

Find a Mentor

The community college I worked for at that time had a laissez-faire relationship with technology, meaning there was no concerted effort to embrace or integrate it, but the college wouldn't stop you from introducing or using it in your courses. I found my mentor by listening to my students. Students talk; if you listen before the start of class or in the campus coffee shop, you will hear their opinions on just about everything, including faculty. On a community college campus, there is a great variety of learners, including age and experience, and their perspectives on the value of their professors are always interesting, if not ultimately valuable. Students value professors who take an active role in their learning, who engage them, who challenge them, and who inspire them (Umbach & Wawrzynski, 2005). My students talked about my mentor. She was tough but fair, tech savvy, and hip. She used office hours to help students who asked for it; she was respected, and her classes were recommended. So I sought her out after a department meeting, and over coffee we became friends.

No matter how you do it, finding a full-time faculty member who is willing to mentor or assist in some way is an undeniable connection to success in most every field, but especially for freeway faculty (Diegel, 2013), who often feel unsettled, outside the sphere, or even intimidated by academia. Although the majority of full-time instructors (and this was only 8 to 10 years ago) patently avoided new tech (primarily using Blackboard), I found a single instructor who understood its promise in real and practical ways and was willing to assist me in learning it; that one connection made all the difference. (I have since discovered additional mentors who were once freeway faculty, which is indeed valuable, as they fully understand the pitfalls of becoming a stagnant fixture, a professor on cruise control.) I was interested in integrating technology to increase my own time management and the engagement of my students, and I quickly found that my mentor and I had similar views on student-centered approaches to instruction. I cannot imagine my professional success had I not stepped out of my comfort zone and knocked on her office door.

Integrating these technical tools (not just the LMS but the connectivity it gave me to my students by linking to other tools) allowed me to create or join a community of colleagues that was a support system not only for my improving my own skills as a professional but also in managing my time. Being freeway faculty means you spend quality time behind the wheel, which means less time for office hours, less screen time, less time for life in general. Simply put, those who do not develop and maintain superior time management skills do not survive. At my busiest professional semester, I taught eight (!) concurrent courses (online, hybrids, and F-2-F) consisting of four separate preps for three (!) different academic institutions; my husband was genuinely worried that I would have a psychotic episode before Halloween. I not only survived but also thrived. (Although, admittedly, I could not sustain that pace long term!) To survive, you must be honest about the challenges you are facing; your academic institution and administration cannot be expected to guide you, but your community of colleagues can and will keep you on the right road. It's often a personal matter to ask for assistance about anything from dealing with the great variety of administration demands to revising assignment prompts to creating more effective collaborative projects (not to mention grading them!). But I have found that asking is really the hardest part; once you take that risk and share a concern, you'll often find that fellow adjuncts share your drive to continually improve and manage the often overwhelming workload; rare is the adjunct professor who lives on cruise control. They are amazing, often untapped, sources for practical, helpful advice that can ultimately help you manage your time—and your life.

What Comfort Zone?

The only "java" in my life comes in my morning coffee mug. But I eventually became the "go-to girl" in my department when it came to integrating social and digital technologies into my courses because I stepped out of that zone once more (at a new institution) and signed up for a professional development series with a horrendous title along the lines of "Integrating Technology and Pedagogy" or something similar that I would never have enrolled in as a student. I was interested in this idea that I could use technology to help me further my time management skills and was not thinking of this as a "teaching" tool, necessarily, but quickly learned that it could and should be both.

I took advantage of this opportunity in the late summer, which is a time many adjuncts don't look for offerings. Mark your calendar with a reminder to check those websites in July! For many freeway faculty, teaching is a supplementary income (Mueller, Mandernach, & Sanderson, 2013), so any professional development opportunity that can help them in becoming better teachers is generally much appreciated, especially when offered gratis by their institution, which many summer offerings are. This also builds on improving the relationship between the college and the adjunct body, making the latter feel valued. For me, learning how to program a quiz that an LMS will grade for me was like having a small robotic teaching assistant. That's 20 more minutes in a semester I might have to actually relax on a Sunday afternoon, rather than use my time for grading. Having a programmable grade book so that those of us who chose English degrees for a living (rather than, say, math) was a godsend, saving time otherwise spent in grade calculation. I initially learned how to integrate technology to make my life a little easier, but quickly it became more about effective instructional design and course management centered on student learning. If this one tool provided me with (precious) additional time in my day to devote to the craft of teaching, what other tools could I find?

Campuses With Teaching Centers

I was hooked. Once I learned of the professional development offerings at my institution, I carefully combed the listings with the goal of participating once per semester. Where I previously felt like I had to have a decoder ring and special map to find professional development opportunities, I suddenly felt as if they were everywhere. Much of this is due to my institution's hefty financial commitment to faculty development, an impressive example of "small, private schools with teaching, learning, and student development at the heart of [its] enterprise" (Stenerson, Blanchard, Fassiotto, Hernandez, & Muth, 2010). I began keeping the techniques that worked and ditching the ones that didn't. I gave students midterm evaluations *about me and the course* that I collected and pored over to see what was working and was not. Later, the teaching center would do these for any faculty member who requested them to increase both participation and honesty on these survey results. I realize not every campus has a teaching center, but I was teaching for two years before I engaged with any of the programs. Now I look back and think, Why did I wait? The life of a freeway faculty member is not for the weak; you are ridiculously underpaid, and you spend so many hours commuting that your personal life suffers in order to the meet the demands of your professional life. No one will lie to you and say it's an easy ride. Just as you have an emergency kit in the trunk of your car, you have a chest of tools that you use to teach. If you can find new tools that will alleviate some of this freeway stress—tools that will allow you to maintain the job that is your passion—then disconnect your cruise control and make room in the chest for these new tools.

Zombies Can't Dance

I took a professional development course series about blogging. Yes, what I considered the electronic equivalent to letters penned by Grandpa Simpson, blogging. And it opened my eyes to an entirely new way to engage students with the social pedagogical approaches of my teaching. I used the platform in one class, then took my ideas and feedback to another professional development offering about blogs and social media and altered it some more. Then I integrated it into the next semester's course. The Zombies Can't Dance blog (http://digitalcommons.georgiasouthern.edu/sswc/2014/2014/38/) became, in less than one year's time, the greatest tool I'd ever used in the teaching of writing. The teaching center was presenting at the Lilly Conference, a conference series that focuses on evidenced-based teaching and learning, and asked if I would copresent by way of modeling my blog and answering questions. They spoke for 10 minutes, and then I fielded 40 minutes of questions. It was exhilarating! I was suddenly participating in professional development in a way I had not conceived of before that day. I was genuinely adding to the greater conversation versus feeling like I was "merely" learning something new. And the conference itself was a wonderful place to experience new ideas and think of how to use them to better my courses and my practice.

Unparalleled Support

I have been nothing short of blessed to have had, first, amazing colleagues who in lieu of college-provided training helped me achieve professional goals and improve my instructional design and communications and, second, university support for research and the freedom to implement social and digital tools into my course to enhance student learning. My current university provides unparalleled support to adjuncts who seek it, which has allowed me to pursue my research interests, integrate exciting elements into my courses, present at national conferences, submit and publish papers, and receive a grant for research at the Library of Congress, most of which have been paid for by my university! Most freeway faculty are led to believe that these perks of academia are only for full-time professors; however, professional development is about improving education by supporting the ivory tower structure we all love to hate.

I have had professional development assistance with everything from digital tool integrations and research planning to assistance with course redesign (how to take a 15-week course and redesign it for a 4-week mini-semester), but I got there only by starting at the beginning, stepping out of my comfort zone, taking risks, identifying fellow adjuncts, approaching mentors, finding existing programs on campus, and (yes I'll say it) working during summer. The freeway faculty life is not easy, but it is richly rewarding and can be measurably enhanced by using professional development tools. Adjuncts are a tough and resilient mix of adaptability, passion, innovation, momentum, and freedom who are often left to their own devices when it comes to increasing their effectiveness in the classroom. Were it not for outstanding mentors, I would not use technology so effectively in my curriculum; were it not for professional development organization on campus, I would not have developed new innovative teaching methods, much less write about them and share them through presentations at national conferences. Professional development opportunities have made it possible for me to continue in academia; without them I believe I would have hung up my keys for other pursuits long ago.

References

Day, C., & Sachs, J. (2005). *International handbook on the continuing professional development of teachers*. Berkshire, UK: McGraw-Hill Education.

Diegel, B. L. (2013). Perceptions of community college adjunct faculty and division chairpersons: Support, mentoring, and professional development to sustain academic quality. *Community College Journal of Research and Practice, 37*(8), 596–607. doi:10.1080/10668926.2012.720863

Gappa, J. M., & Leslie, D. W. (1993). *The invisible faculty: Improving the status of part-timers in higher education.* San Francisco, CA: Jossey-Bass.

Miller, G. (2014). Presidents, do right by athletes and adjuncts. *The Chronicle of Higher Education, 60*(39), 25.

Mueller, B., Mandernach, B. J., & Sanderson, K. (2013). Adjunct versus full-time faculty: Comparison of student outcomes in the online classroom. *Journal of Online Learning and Teaching, 9*(3), 341–352. Retrieved from http://jolt.merlot .org/vol9no3/mueller_0913.htm

Stenerson, J., Blanchard, L., Fassiotto, M., Hernandez, M., & Muth, A. (2010). The role of adjuncts in the professoriate. *Peer Review, 12*(3). Retrieved from https:// www.aacu.org/publications-research/periodicals/role-adjuncts-professoriate

Umbach, P. D., & Wawrzynski, M. R. (2005). Faculty do matter: The role of college faculty in student learning and engagement. *Research in Higher Education, 46,* 153–184. Retrieved from http://www.jstor.org/stable/40197351

5

We Know We Have Lost

Contingency, Grieving, and Imagination

Chris Potts

Disconnected

I'd just returned from the Conference on College Composition and Communication (CCCC) in Indianapolis. I was flush with excitement, eager to get back into the classroom to apply what I'd learned, and excited to share my experiences with colleagues. But mingled with that enthusiasm was a sense of loss I found difficult to communicate. I didn't know what I'd lost exactly, but I knew when I first felt it.

One of the last panels I attended at CCCC dealt with multimodality. One presenter described how he'd facilitated a unique faculty training program that situated composition and literature instructors as coexperimenters tasked with the challenge of working collaboratively to develop "sonic compositions"—strange things to the uninitiated. The thinking went that faculty—tenured and contingent—might let down their guard and grow together into new and shared insights, common prompts and assessment tools, and perhaps even collaborative research projects when challenged to explore new ground by developing assignments that would allow students to create compositions leveraging the affordances of sound. Now, I'd been accustomed to acknowledging the poverty of my own pedagogy at conferences—it stings, but we go, many of us, to be stung and moved to change. Never, though, had I been forced to confront the relative poverty of my situation as a lecturer in my department. Stings are stings, and loss is loss.

Once, a department secretary stopped me in the hallway because a tenured faculty member had been "insulted" to find a flyer (not of my making, by the way) announcing a workshop to be given by "*Professor* Christopher Potts." "He wanted me to remind you," she reported, carrying over in her tone some of the contempt inherent in the message, "you're *not* a professor." It stung. I would have seemed petulant had I told her the truth that I have always *disallowed* students to call me professor, already keenly aware of my second-class status. I didn't need to be publicly shamed; I'd long since learned to be grateful just to have a position, never mind a vaunted title. In this degraded condition of powerlessness and voicelessness (Jacobe, 2006), it never occurred to me to yearn for a robust training program or a warm nurturing collegial environment such as the one the presenter described. We cannot make what we cannot imagine, and our imagination is degraded by insecurity, low pay, and high course loads. I wonder: Were responsibility for our condition shared more equally, were we permitted to share more equally in the responsibility of shaping the university, were we empowered to imagine, what a force we might be!

I went home from CCCC newly aware of having lost years of the collegiality I'd experienced at the conference and, worse, the capacity to imagine it in my home environment. I commiserated with one of my colleagues from down the hall, an old friend I'd tutored with in a previous life. This made sense, this choice of an old friend to confide in; in my department, previous association is the primary basis for collegiality. My department offers no training program to foster faculty relationships through creative problem-based training and assessment modules, excludes adjunct faculty from department meetings, and rarely holds faculty mixers. Indeed, the only facilitated social environment for faculty in my department is the biannual Exit/Comp Co-op exam scoring session, and instructors attend these either because they must or because they want extra cash. The goal is to leave, not to commune. This pattern of disengagement, my colleague and I decided, must be addressed. We also assumed the department would do nothing to address it. It fell to us. He teased me, as he's wont to do, insisting that I didn't have the courage to invite my colleagues to the "best practices workshop" we'd begun to outline in that fevered discussion. So I went to my office immediately, and I did it—mostly to spite him.

Communion and Commiseration

What happened after that surprised me. I regretted sending the e-mail blast immediately. My earnestness offended the already well-developed cynicism that had begun to calcify in me after the disappointment of returning home to a department that seemed aloof to professional development, and I assumed it would offend my older and more cynical colleagues all the more. I felt overeager, presumptuous, vulnerable. Fancy inviting seasoned veterans to a "best practices workshop"! What gall. I felt like Bono crooning the lyrics to

All I Want is You (U2, 1988) to a throng of hipsters in ironic T-shirts designed to deflect and dismiss as clichéd the messages of hope and love. Then, within minutes, the replies started coming in. I opened each with great apprehension, and each time I felt more . . . encouraged. My expression of excitement was not deflected or dismissed (though I was teased some by my office mate); instead, it was returned. And many times over.

Most of my colleagues never replied to the e-mail. Two of the tenured faculty were apologetic: They loved the idea but could not attend a workshop on Fridays (the only day I imagined could work for most of us). A couple of the lecturers taught on Fridays but said they'd try for the next semester. Several others complained that, as much as they'd like to attend, they were already severely underpaid and overworked. One veteran adjunct seemed aghast that in the midst of a labor struggle I'd propose doing *extra* work for no pay.

Insecurity, Low Pay, High Course Loads

On my campus, these problems were particularly acute. Many of us lecturers had learned only months before that we'd been misclassified, hired in at a pay rate incommensurate with our degree and/or experience. A small group of lecturers were astute enough to notice and courageous enough to fight. When my e-mail blast went out, our department chair had just taken on our cause, and our dean had just deflected or absorbed or ignored the first volleys of the dispute. Our union, the California Faculty Association, long an advocate for contingent faculty (Berry & Hoffman, 2008), and the chair of the academic senate had yet to learn of our latest grievance. Nonetheless, given the insecurity, the low pay, the high workload, and a prevailing sense that these conditions were immutable, eight instructors promised to come in on a Friday two weeks later for two hours to discuss praxis, and six actually did!

The group met three or four times that semester. These were informal affairs. Sure, I recommended themes to address, but, like good composition instructors, we assiduously ignored them in ways we'd punish our students severely for. We would not be constrained. Our conversations were meandering, shuttling among uncritical tirades bemoaning the detachment of young people; deeply incisive theoretical debates about modalities and agency; and practical reflections on essay prompts, syllabi construction, and classroom management. Always, though, these discussions were haunted and animated by insecurity, low pay, and high course loads. It was therapeutic to talk about it out in the open. We bonded over it. Indeed, these threats to our collective imagination seemed less acute the more we met. We were making up for what we'd lost. But we still had difficulty imagining what we could accomplish, difficulty imagining the power latent in our community.

Small projects came out of these early meetings—modest collaborations. This instructor would share a prompt with that one, or a lesson, or a text. But the real project was *us*: building a basis for collegiality other than prior association. We did this by creating a liminal space within and beyond the department to challenge the cynicism and isolation imposed on us by our second-class status within and beyond the department. Looking back, there was an elegant symmetry to it. And who would imagine that we, with that modest goal, would serve as a model for a newly installed administration looking to foster faculty relationships and collaborations across disciplines through a rebuilt Faculty Development Center? But that's what happened. Our time had come.

The next semester, our meetings were held and facilitated through the Faculty Development Center and open to faculty members from all disciplines. Our challenge now was to discuss writing in a manner accessible to faculty from all departments. Our first meeting that spring was accompanied by some fanfare. It was attended by the dean of undergraduate studies, the chair of the Academic Senate, a tenured professor from the Department of Business and Administration, the assistant director of the Toro Learning Center, several supplemental instructors, and four stalwart lecturers from the English Department eager to share their work. It was a lively and inspiring session. One of the lecturers in attendance—you'll remember him—had once been aghast that we would choose to do extra work for free. I was surprised and excited to have him present to us—surprised because he was sweet enough not to condemn us for work he once deemed out of line and humble enough to change his mind. As it turned out, he had more surprises in store than we could have imagined. Indeed, his presentation might well have turned the tide of the labor dispute that, by that time, had been ongoing for the better part of a year with little progress to show for adjuncts.

Larry, we'll call him, presented an innocuous grammar lesson. It was silly and self-deprecating, and he had us all giggling. But like all of our discussions, it was haunted, animated by insecurity, low pay, and overwork. So when the senate chair posed an equally innocuous question about the time it takes to assess assignments like the one discussed, the floodgates, shuddering against the tide, released a torrent of insecurity. Larry parlayed the question about time into an opportunity to fulminate against the administration's inaction on the issue of misclassification. Unflappable, the senate chair probed deeper. He was unaware of our ongoing battle, and he vowed to take our concerns to the Academic Senate. But just as important, he recognized that adjuncts require a safe space to commiserate, and our workshop was that space. He understood that if we are to build robust adjunct communities, contingent faculty must first sense that responsibility for their condition— not just student success—is shared.

Much good came of that first Faculty Development Center best practices workshop. First, the senate chair acted decisively as he had promised, banding together with fellow senators to insist that our new president redress the wrongs of previous administrations and reclassify misclassified adjuncts. Second, the undergraduate dean, recognizing the as-yet untapped resource an energized adjunct community could provide for campus initiatives, risked investing in contingent faculty. I received the e-mail from the dean at the end of that same semester. She'd invited me, along with two other adjuncts, to accompany herself and a tenured faculty member from my department to the Association of American Colleges & Universities' Institute for Integrative Learning to be held at California State University, Fullerton, that summer. As a team, we were tasked with the challenge of developing "innovative interdisciplinary teaching, learning, and assessment practices" (Association of American Colleges & Universities, 2014). In our case that meant developing a proposal for an integrative *high-impact practice*-infused (HIP-infused) first-year writing experience to pitch to the vice provost back home. A void filled in me. Just as the presenter at the CCCC had described, we grew together, sharing the responsibility of developing not only the course but also a way to leverage the experience of adjuncts to make the course real and effective.

Anger, Bargaining, Denial

The following fall, I was asked to lead a faculty learning community (FLC), tasked with developing syllabi, assignments, and assessment tools for the new integrative, HIP-infused first-year research writing course. This FLC, modeled after our best practices workshop, would be the first to run through the reinvigorated Faculty Development Center and, as it turned out, the only one made up entirely of adjuncts. Twelve of us applied to meet five times in the fall to imagine the course together. Some of us would also have the opportunity to implement the course the following spring. Our first meeting went smoothly. It was good to be together. A few of the participants were holdovers from the early days of the best practices workshop. Most were new to me. I had literally never seen them, but I'd heard their names from students, heard stories about them that intrigued me. We were excited to see what we'd come up with.

Two weeks later we came back together. It was an intense session. Though we'd begun by honoring two of the participants for their role in bringing about a newly ratified California Faculty Association contract strongly favoring adjuncts and taking steps to redress the wrongs of misclassification, it was clear that we were still focused on what we had lost. How, one participant asked, can *they* expect us to read all these articles and books when we have so many papers to grade? How, asked another, can *they* expect us to develop a whole new assignment mid-semester? These "deliverables" (the course syllabus, the key HIP-infused assignment, and the assessment tool), some said, were totally unreasonable. The gall! Here I was again, feeling overeager, presumptuous, vulnerable. Only this time it wasn't just my imagination. I'd already lost control. And it was my fault: I wanted to ignore labor issues and move on. I organized the expression of gratitude at the beginning of the session in part to be a symbolic hand-washing gesture, a reframing device. But there would be no moving on.

Insecurity, Low Pay, High Course Loads Redux

The word *they* never just rolled off the tongue in our sessions; it was spat into the room like venom no matter how often it was used. It was a catchall term designating tenured faculty in our department (especially them) and administrators alike. I don't see *them* in here delivering these "deliverables," one participant quipped. What do *they* want? We can't fail to implement these designs, or *they* won't pay us. *They* care only about numbers, results. It seemed childish to me, and small and cynical, this us-versus-them game. But I had yet to fully acknowledge the ways in which "second-class treatment is internalized variously and results in fear, anger, lack of self-confidence and esteem, and general insecurity" (Berry & Hoffman, 2008, p. 30). I was still in denial; my colleagues had already moved into the anger phase of grief.

Twice in the course of the semester, FLC facilitators met with a trainer, someone with extensive experience running FLCs. She was there to troubleshoot, to offer advice. I was eager to share our story, to learn what I'd done wrong, what I could do better to make my community cohere and produce as it was supposed to. I did, and I was shocked by her response: She'd never heard of anything like what I was describing before, she said. It sounded like laziness to her—a crass money grab by unenthusiastic, careless hacks. Now it was my turn to be aghast. In essence, her response was an eyes-covered, ears-plugged denial of the possibility that labor issues and insecurity can disrupt learning communities.

Acceptance

At the final training meeting, the trainer asked me to speak again. She meant to frame our story as a failure, a cautionary tale. But we hadn't failed. Once I'd learned to translate anger as fear, I was capable of being empathetic, able to commiserate again, able to be reassuring. I told the story of the session when we realized as a group that this shadowy *they* we kept spitting out had *invested* in us. They *wanted* our input. They *believed* in us. They had *shared* with us responsibility for their initiatives, their grand schemes. They had *empowered* us to design, pilot, and assess a new course. Given all that we had lost, it had just been difficult to imagine being an integral part of our university. I was like Bono again, crooning about there being no them, only us (U2, 2014). It looks silly on the page, but it's what we needed to hear.

Adjunct communities can build around collective loss, sure. But that goes only so far. To leverage the power latent in the collective experience of that insecure, underpaid, overworked class of instructors that powers our institutions of higher learning, the secure ones must share responsibility for adjuncts' condition and allow them to share responsibility for the grand design of those institutions. This might mean sharing the title of "professor" with contingent faculty (McGrew & Untener, 2010) or granting them a "voice in governance" (Anonymous, 2009) or inviting them to collaborate. Whatever form it takes, this sharing of responsibility between contingent and noncontingent faculty and administrators is the essence of a new collegiality in an era when adjuncts teach heavier loads than tenured faculty (Anonymous, 2009) and bear the greatest share of the burden to facilitate student leaning, "which decreases in an environment with unsupported, disconnected, and disenfranchised faculty members" (McGrew & Untener, 2010, p. 44). We know what we have lost; now let us look to what we gain by bringing adjuncts into the fold.

References

Anonymous. (2009). The unhappy experience of contingent faculty. *Academe, 95*(6), 22–25. Retrieved from http://www.jstor.org/stable/20694589

Association of American Colleges & Universities. (2014). 2014 Institute on Integrative Learning and the Departments. Retrieved from https://www.aacu.org/summerinstitutes/ild/2014

Berry, J., & Hoffman, E. (2008). Including contingent faculty in governance. *Academe, 94*(6), 29–31. Retrieved from http://www.jstor.org/stable/40253268

Jacobe, M. (2006). Contingent faculty across the disciplines. *Academe, 92*(6), 43–49. doi:10.2307/40253524

McGrew, H., & Untener, J. (2010). A primer on improving faculty conditions. *Academe, 96*(4), 43–45. Retrieved from http://www.jstor.org/stable/20744595

U2. (1988). All I want is you. On *Rattle and hum*. London, UK: Island Records.

U2. (2014). There is no them, only us. On *Songs of innocence*. London, UK Island Records.

6

Using a Community of Practice to Enhance the Adjunct Experience

Paul G. Putman and Bridget A. Kriner

Feelings of isolation and a sense of disconnection are all-too-common experiences for adjunct faculty (Ferguson & Shaw, 2013; Rhoades, 2013). Adjunct faculty often must balance schedules that include a full-time position outside of teaching or may include multiple courses taught at one or more institutions. As teaching is not necessarily their primary focus, and they may not have as much time to commit to teaching as their full-time counterparts, adjunct teaching quality can be a concern (Baker, 2014). Grubb and colleagues (1999) noted that "good teachers were more likely to be strongly connected with other faculty" and that "without contact among colleagues, there are few discussions about instruction, no forums where the special pedagogical problems of community college can be debated and resolved" (p. 42). Adjuncts are integral to higher education yet too often are simultaneously held at arm's length from the institutions at which they teach and are less connected than full-time professors (Ferguson & Shaw, 2013). Given the temporary nature of the adjunct role, as well as the typical lack of a physical office or gathering space, it can be challenging to build lasting connections to the institution and difficult to find other adjunct faculty. In our experience, creating communities of adjuncts can be beneficial in many ways, although we focus on the fact that these communities (a) reduce feelings of isolation, (b) help adjuncts learn best teaching practices, and (c) support collaboration on research.

In this chapter, we (two adjunct faculty members teaching at different local institutions; one at a four-year public institution and the other at a two-year community college) discuss our experiences and how we became connected through a *community of practice* (CoP) that we helped form several years ago during a doctoral seminar. That group continues to meet on a regular basis. In this chapter, we share our story of how that community was developed and continues to improve our practice as instructors and scholars. We also share several recommendations for finding and creating communities of adjunct faculty.

Paul's Experience

Although I work full-time in a field outside of education, I was keen to maintain some connection to academia after graduation and was excited when my dissertation chair extended the offer to coteach a course with her. I graduated with my PhD from a public research institution in the Midwest in spring, I cotaught an advanced doctoral seminar that fall (for no pay and off the books so to speak) and the following spring I began teaching as a part-time instructor (i.e., adjunct), teaching one master's-level course during the spring semester and one during the summer semester. I had not previously realized how isolating being an adjunct can be and how quickly one can become disconnected from research and writing. The CoP has allowed me the opportunity to remain active in those activities, which otherwise would likely have atrophied because of disuse. One of the biggest takeaways for me was the peer mentoring that emerged from this process. This helped me, as an adjunct, dispel the feeling of isolation that can emerge and helped me maintain progress with my research agenda as well. It has also provided insight into a diverse set of ideas and topics that I would otherwise have missed.

Bridget's Experience

I had worked as an adjunct at a neighboring community college for several years prior to enrolling in the doctoral program in adult education at Cleveland State University where the CoP initially formed. As a first-year doctoral student, I was overwhelmed by the volume of course work as well as the prospect of learning how to submit work for publication, create conference proposals, and apply for academic jobs. At the time that I began working on my doctorate, I had been teaching composition and developmental English at a community college for several years. I was functioning in two worlds, as both a full-time doctoral student and a part-time faculty member.

The CoP has provided great support for me as both an adjunct and a doctoral student. It has allowed me to develop a model of a CoP that I have introduced in my own classes; it also guided me toward developing a plan for my doctoral research. The CoP has been both a tool that has allowed me to develop professionally and a teaching practice that I have used in my classes. The nature of a CoP allows it to be flexible to meet the changing needs of an adjunct faculty member, a position that is prone to sudden changes. Thus, a good CoP allows members to continually adapt to meet changing needs as adjuncts.

Defining *Communities of Practice*

"Professional development is important in an era where individuals have multiple careers instead of progressive positions" (Monaghan, 2011, p. 429). One way to approach professional development is through self-direction, in which the adjunct takes responsibility for her or his own development. CoPs combine self-directed learning with collaborative learning. In their seminal work on situated learning, Lave and Wenger (1991) argued that learning was not the mere acquisition of skills or accumulation of knowledge. Instead, they conceptualized learning as a social process in which learners are situated in CoPs, groups of people who share a common development goal. CoPs allow for learning to be situated in a practical context, which differentiates it from other types of learning theory or practice. Although Lave and Wenger do not claim to have created the CoP model, they are largely credited with ascribing the term *community of practice* to situated learning contexts, which are common across a variety of academic and professional disciplines.

Expanding on the work he did with Lave, Wenger (1999) further developed the CoP model. He argued that learning is not an activity that can be separated from other situations and life experiences. Wenger argued for a model of learning he called a "social theory of learning," which encompasses dimensions of learning such as social structure, collectivity, practice, meaning, situated experience, power, identity, and subjectivity. In essence, Wenger did not propose that this theory of learning should replace other models of learning but rather proposed that his model is an attempt to better understand how learning operates with the social structure.

Kim and Merriam (2010) reiterated the point that learning is not an individual activity but one that is set within social practices and relationships or situated learning. As adults participate in a CoP, their identities are developed and negotiated based on the context of the situation; participants may experience increased self-efficacy, higher self-esteem, and fewer feelings of marginalization in the larger community.

Zimitat (2007) explained that a CoP "describes social mechanisms by which novices are inducted into expert ways of knowing, thinking, and reasoning in their professional or practice circle" (p. 322). As such, a CoP allows space for experts and novices to interact professionally and intentionally. It is this intentional interaction outside of formal institutional programming that creates the opportunity for growth and development. Furthermore, Webb, Wong, and Hubball (2013) argued explicitly for the value of a CoP for adjunct faculty. Given the conditions that often accompany a role as an adjunct, "a situated and flexible community of practice thus promotes feelings of inclusion, respect, and support for adjunct faculty's contributions" (p. 233).

CoP Formation

Our CoP was established several years ago during a doctoral seminar course (Kriner, Coffman, Adkisson, Putman, & Monaghan, 2015). Paul served as a coinstructor for the course, having recently finished his PhD work, and Bridget was in the beginning of her doctoral studies. The group also includes one full-time faculty member and two other doctoral students and has been meeting monthly for nearly three years. The course instructor had used the CoP approach in many of her graduate classes. As such, she approached the course asking students to guide the course by making decisions about what aspects of the curriculum *we* would explore and in what way *we* would explore them.

At its core, the CoP approach is egalitarian in nature. Bridget noted,

> Although it was not her explicit intention at the time, this approach allowed the bonds of the CoP to be forged across hierarchical levels that might have been prohibitive in other contexts (e.g., different levels within the doctoral program, professor–student, etc. . . .). Because the class functioned as a group of colleagues, it was able to effectively segue beyond the course.

Once the semester ended, the group continued to meet on a regular basis in order to complete research projects that were started during the previous semester. Eventually, the group evolved in such a way that we now meet regularly to provide professional support to each other in each of our various academic pursuits.

What CoP Has Meant for Bridget

My colleagues have helped me in so many ways with my work. They have provided support to me in my own academic job search, helped me think through various aspects of my dissertation proposal, and helped me prepare for my comprehensive exams. Because being an adjunct faculty member can be a very isolating experience, it has been extraordinarily beneficial for me to participate in this CoP. The CoP has helped me think through the way that I approach teaching my courses and how I evaluate student work. I am able to find valuable support for my teaching practice in my colleagues, despite the fact that I am the only one who teaches in the discipline of college English within the group. The solid foundation in the scholarly discipline of adult education gives the group a focus that has allowed me to develop as an educator.

What CoP Has Meant for Paul

The concept of a community of adjuncts raises the question, "To what end?" In my thinking, a community within the academic program has value for both curriculum continuity and student support. Ideally it can help improve teaching practice as well. However, just as important to me is the connection to the scholarly pursuit of research and writing. Without the frame of an academic program, the act of continuing research and writing is nebulous at best, and the CoP has filled the need I have for contributing to the literature and remaining intellectually stimulated through the sharing of research and ideas.

Advice for Finding or Building a Community of Adjuncts

We recognize that the approach that we took in forming our CoP is not necessarily a path that could be replicated easily by a group of adjuncts looking to participate in a CoP as a way to develop a community of professional support; nonetheless, it is an example of how a CoP can provide excellent professional support to a group of adjuncts. It is a model that is open-ended, so it can be used to foster whatever professional development agenda the group of adjunct faculty might have.

In our experience, institutions do not go too far out of their way to help adjunct faculty connect to the institution or to other faculty. Often, the impetus is placed on the adjunct faculty who "must integrate into the existing learning community of the institution" (Ferguson & Shaw, 2013, p. 7). As you seek to connect to other faculty members, we recommend starting with your program, department, or college; connecting with institution-wide resources; and, if all else fails, reaching out on your own. The first point of connection will likely be the program or department within which you are teaching. Perhaps it begins with your chair or dean hosting an orientation session or a "meet the faculty" session. Anecdotally, we are seeing institutions becoming increasingly aware of the need to more fully incorporate adjunct

faculty into the fabric of the university or college as they recognize the importance of adjunct faculty to the mission of the institution and the impact of
isolation on retention. Savvy deans and department chairs recognize that
providing opportunities for socialization and connection are important, as
adjuncts may not be likely to reach out to other adjuncts or full-time faculty
members of their own accord. Pearch and Marutz (2005) presented socialization as one important component of retaining adjunct faculty and listed
several event examples for consideration ranging from inclusion in existing
college celebrations and ceremonies to an all-faculty dinner. A faculty dinner,
professional development seminar, or reception with the dean could all be
great venues for adjunct faculty to meet each other. Providing time during an
event for adjunct faculty to coalesce around topics of interest could lay the
foundation for continued conversation and perhaps the emergence of a CoP.
A departmental electronic mailing list or other online shared space could
also spark questions and conversations leading to a deeper working conversation (i.e., "Does anyone know anything about this new online learning platform?" "No, but I'd love to get together to talk about it and figure it out.").

Ideally, your institution is taking the advice of Meixner, Kruck, and Madden
(2010), who emphasized the importance of communication and outreach to
adjuncts. If there is not a robust flow of communication and outreach, see
if you can obtain a list of adjuncts in your department and send out an
invitation to meet. Because many adjuncts have complex workloads, consider online options (particularly asynchronous ones) as a viable option. The
institution may have an office of adjunct services or similar program, which
would also be a natural place to begin. If one of your goals is professional
development, look to your center for faculty or teaching excellence and/or
workshops offered to faculty as places to connect. You may have to do some
work to get on mailing lists, but workshops are a great place to find like-
minded adjuncts. Creating a CoP with a group of adjuncts could start with
something as simple as inviting the other adjuncts in a discipline or department to an informal meeting over coffee. Start by sharing experiences as
adjuncts; talk about career or teaching goals. Find some common ground.

If the group collectively develops some shared goals, then a second meeting can grow into an ongoing touch point. If you are part of a small program
or department, approaching this at the division or college level might be the
best tactic. You can create your own connection through a CoP or other con-
figuration that meets the needs of your group. The beauty of a CoP is that it
does not require that its members adhere to any one method of formation,
so any starting place can be workable to form one. A CoP does not even have
to be limited to adjuncts at one institution or in one discipline. What has
worked well in our CoP is that we have been able to shift our focus as we

moved away from our initial shared experience as students and instructors to more of a peer group that provides support for ongoing research and professional development endeavors. Paul noted,

> We have supported each other through sharing teaching, learning, and writing challenges and joys. We have collaborated on a national conference presentation and paper and recently had our first collective journal article published.

For adjuncts who share similar backgrounds or goals, a CoP can provide great support. Essentially, a CoP is an excellent model from which a community of adjuncts can be built. As we have experienced firsthand, a CoP model offers its participants a great deal of flexibility to build a community to meet individual development needs and goals. The value of a CoP for creating connections among adjunct faculty is in making a space to share experiences with those who have common professional experiences and/or who are moving toward a common professional goal.

References

Baker, B. (2014). The end of the academy? *Bioscience, 64*(8), 647–652.

Ferguson, K., & Shaw, M. (2013). Evaluation of adjunct instructor workload and employment conditions in higher education. *Journal of Online Higher Education, 4*(5). Retrieved from http://www.theelearninginstitute.org/journal_pdf/JOHE%20-%20Evaluation%20of%20Adjunct%20Instructor%20Workload%20and%20Employment%20Conditions%20in%20Higher%20Education.pdf

Grubb, W. N., Worthen, H., Byrd, B., Webb, E., Badway, N., Case, C., Goto, S., & Villenueve, J. C. (1999). *Honored but invisible: An inside look at teaching in community colleges.* New York, NY: Routledge.

Kim, Y. S., & Merriam, S. B. (2010). Situated learning and identity development in Korean older adults' computer classroom. *Adult Education Quarterly, 60*(5), 438–455. doi:10.1177/0741713610363019

Kriner, B. A., Coffman, K. A., Adkisson, A. C., Putman, P. G., & Monaghan, C. H. (2015). From students to scholars: The transformative power of communities of practice. *Adult Learning, 26,* 73–80. doi:10.1177/1045159515573021

Lave, J., & Wenger, E. (1991). *Situated learning: Legitimate peripheral participation.* New York, NY: Cambridge University Press.

Meixner, C., Kruck, S. E., & Madden, L. T. (2010). Inclusion of part-time faculty for the benefit of faculty and students. *College Teaching, 58*(4), 141–147. doi:10.1080/87567555.2010.484032

Monaghan, C. (2011). Communities of practice: A learning strategy for management education. *Journal of Management Education, 35*(3), 428–453. doi:10.1177/1052562910387536

Pearch, W. J., & Marutz, L. (2005). Retention of adjunct faculty in community colleges. *Community College Enterprise, 11*(1), 29–44. Retrieved from https://www.questia.com/library/journal/1P3-850866761/retention-of-adjunct-faculty-in-community-colleges

Rhoades, G. (2013, Fall). Disruptive innovations for adjunct faculty: Common sense for the common good. *Thought and Action, 29,* 71–86. Retrieved from http://www.nea.org/assets/docs/HE/k-pg71_TA2013Rhoades_SF.pdf

Webb, A. S., Wong, T. J., & Hubball, H. T. (2013). Professional development for adjunct teaching faculty in a research-intensive university: Engagement in scholarly approaches to teaching and learning. *International Journal of Teaching and Learning in Higher Education, 25,* 231–238. Retrieved from http://www.isetl.org/ijtlhe/pdf/IJTLHE1520.pdf

Wenger, E. (1999). *Communities of practice: Learning, meaning, and identity.* Cambridge, UK: Cambridge University Press.

Zimitat, C. (2007). Capturing community of practice knowledge for student learning. *Innovations in Education and Teaching International, 44*(3), 321–330. doi:10.1080/14703290701486753

Part Two

Adjunct Faculty Development: Personnel and Programs

7

A Survey of Adjunct Faculty Developers

Kimberly Smith and Roy Fuller

Methods

To understand the current state of adjunct faculty development, we conducted a survey to collect the views of faculty developers who offer programs specifically in support of adjunct faculty (see the appendix for the complete survey). "Exploring the State of Adjunct Faculty Development: A Survey of Faculty Developers" sought answers to the following:

- What are the demographics of those engaged in adjunct faculty development, including the titles and/or roles they serve in faculty development; how long have they worked in the field; and what is the structure of their institution's faculty development offerings?
- How do adjunct faculty participate in their programs, and what percentage of their program participants are adjunct faculty?
- What are the goals and purposes of their current faculty development programs, the factors that have influenced their program decisions, and the types of incentives offered to adjunct faculty who participate in their programs?
- What is the presence of adjunct organizations and unions at their institutions, and to what extent are adjunct faculty involved in faculty governance?

The survey also included a series of open-ended questions where developers were asked to share what they are doing well in adjunct development, what they would want to do, and what they believe are the most significant challenges in supporting adjunct faculty.

The comments collected through the survey revealed both a wide range in the level of support for adjunct faculty development and much consensus on the challenges of serving this growing segment of the academic workforce.

Survey Deployment

Unlike researchers using earlier surveys of faculty development that targeted all faculty developers (Sorcinelli, Austin, Eddy, & Beach, 2006), we were interested in reaching persons who are specifically involved in adjunct faculty development. We deployed the survey through the Professional and Organizational Development Network in Higher Education (POD Network), which is the largest professional organization for faculty developers in higher education. The survey was sent to the POD Network electronic mailing list, which at the time of deployment in August 2015 had 2,811 recipients. The survey invitation was also sent to members of the Service Employees International Union (SEIU) Local 509 in Massachusetts, which includes 3,400 part- and full-time faculty in the greater Boston area. The e-mail invitation to participate also invited persons to share the invitation with colleagues who work in adjunct faculty development. The survey was open to participants for approximately seven weeks, from August 12, 2015, to October 1, 2015. We received 80 responses.

Respondent Demographics

The faculty developer survey asked respondents to indicate their institution's type according to the 2010 Carnegie classification system. Table 7.1 shows the number and percentage of total respondents for each category.

Because the POD Network has many members from large universities, most of which have established faculty development programs, the number of respondents from doctoral-granting institutions (40%) is higher than the representation of such institutions nationally (7%), whereas the number of

TABLE 7.1
Respondents by Institutional Type, 2010 Carnegie Classification

2010 Carnegie Classification	n	Percentage (%)
Associate's Colleges	14	17.50
Doctorate-Granting Universities	32	40.00
Master's Colleges and Universities	16	20.00
Baccalaureate Colleges	8	10.00
Special Focus Institutions	1	1.25
Tribal Colleges	1	1.25
Other	8	10.00

respondents from associate's colleges (17.5%) is lower than the representation of such institutions nationally (32%). Similar findings were observed by Sorcinelli and colleagues (2006), who speculated that the lower representation from community colleges may be due to many community college developers belonging to the National Council for Staff, Program, and Organizational Development (NCSPOD) rather than the POD Network. Although NCSPOD is no longer an active organization, many community college developers do belong to the National Institute for Staff and Organizational Development (NISOD), which offers support for administrators and developers at community and technical colleges in the United States.

Of our 80 respondents, 53 (66.25%) were at public institutions, whereas 27 (33.75%) were affiliated with private institutions. Forty-six respondents (57.50%) had a faculty appointment, and 34 respondents (42.50%) did not. While 81.25% of respondents indicated they were employed full-time (n = 65), a significant percentage (18.75%) indicated they were part-time (n = 15). In regard to length of service in faculty development, the range was between 1 year and 24 years. We also asked respondents to indicate which roles they filled within their institutions (see Table 7.2). Respondents were able to select more than one option to indicate multiple roles. Percentages indicate that of the total number of respondents (N = 80).

We asked respondents to identify their institution's faculty development structure. Our categories followed those used by Sorcinelli and colleagues (2006), and our results were fairly similar. Respondents were asked to best

TABLE 7.2
All Titles or Roles of Respondents

Title or Role	n	Percentage (%)
Director	34	42.50
Assistant/Associate Director	12	15.00
Program Coordinator	11	13.75
Technology Coordinator	2	2.50
Senior-Level Administrator	6	7.50
Instructional Development Consultant	12	15.00
Faculty Member	34	42.50
Other	8	10.00

TABLE 7.3
Faculty Development by Organizational Structure

Faculty Development Structure	n = 79	Percentage (%)
A centralized unit with dedicated staff	52	65.82
An individual faculty member charged with supporting faculty development	14	17.72
A committee charged with supporting faculty development	6	7.59
A "clearinghouse" for programs and offerings	1	1.26
Other	6	7.59

describe their structure using the following categories: a centralized unit with dedicated staff that offers a range of faculty development programs, an individual faculty member or administrator charged with supporting faculty development, a committee charged with supporting faculty development, a "clearinghouse" for programs and offerings, or another type of arrangement not listed (see Table 7.3).

Although we do not claim that our pool of respondents represents the scope and proportion of adjunct faculty development programs in the United States, we do believe the results shed light on the current state of adjunct faculty development and highlight the ongoing needs of developers who serve the adjunct faculty population.

Data Analysis

Quantitative items were analyzed according to the percentage of respondents who answered a question in a particular manner. Percentages of respondents refer to the percentage of total survey respondents (N = 80) except where noted otherwise. Percentages are reported out to two decimal places. Independent t-tests were run to find correlations among survey respondents according to various demographic groupings. Few statistically significant correlations were found. Those relationships found to be statistically significant are reported in the findings.

In addition to quantitative items, the survey included several open-ended questions. The qualitative data gathered from these questions were analyzed in three cycles. Open coding was used for the first cycle to identify major common themes. The open codes and identified themes were used to develop a codebook for each individual, open-ended question. This was followed by a second cycle in which each individual qualitative survey item was analyzed using pattern coding to identify nuances among the themes and to provide a sense of the frequency with which various topics were mentioned. The third cycle used pattern coding to compare responses from all qualitative items in order to identify themes that ran throughout the survey responses. The pattern coding process produced three major overarching themes: institutional culture, strategies for adjunct professional development, and challenges in supporting adjunct faculty. Major themes and subthemes are described in the findings. Actual survey responses are included where relevant.

Findings

Institutional Culture

Survey responses repeatedly provided insight into respondents' perspectives of the cultures of their institutions. Institutional culture, as it relates to attitudes about and treatment of adjunct faculty, appears to cover a broad spectrum. Some survey respondents felt that their institution was supportive and inclusive of adjunct faculty, whereas others described institutions that treated adjunct faculty as second-class members of the college or university.

The degree to which an institution includes adjunct faculty in decision-making processes can be particularly telling of overall attitudes about adjuncts; thus, survey respondents were asked whether their faculty governance structure allows for the direct participation of adjunct faculty. The 41.25% of survey respondents who indicated that their faculty governance structure allowed for direct participation of adjunct faculty were asked to further articulate how adjuncts were included in governance. Because each respondent highlighted different aspects of his or her faculty governance structure, it is not possible to reveal a meaningful sense of how the responses compared to one another, but the data give us a sense of the array of ways that adjunct faculty are included in the institutional governance system. Eight respondents stated that adjunct faculty members had voting representation on an institution-wide or departmental governing body. At other institutions, one or more adjunct representatives are granted opportunities to give voice to adjunct concerns, but they do not have voting privileges. Several institutions set aside a number of seats on institutional governing bodies specifically for adjunct or part-time faculty. Two respondents mentioned unions as the primary means for adjunct representation on their campus. Two respondents indicated that there was a distinction in opportunity to participate in governance between adjunct faculty who worked full-time and those who worked part-time:

> Full-time NTT [non-tenure-track] faculty have equal roles as tenure-track
> faculty in governance, but part-time faculty have very limited roles.

Additional comments throughout the survey suggested that institutions
should allow for greater opportunities for adjuncts to have a voice, whether
through participation in governance or through opportunities to express their
concerns to administrators ($n = 9$).

Providing accessible spaces for adjunct faculty to participate in institutional governance may be one of the best possible ways to let them know they
are valued and make them feel included. However, many faculty developers
will have limited control over this aspect of their institutional culture. Faculty
developers can most readily contribute to the culture of adjunct inclusion by
ensuring that adjunct faculty are welcome and included in faculty development programs and services offered by the institution. Sixty survey respondents (75%) stated that part-time faculty were a primary audience for their
institution's faculty development programs and services. Nearly all respondents (96.25%) indicated that adjunct faculty participate in their institution's
faculty development programs or services. All faculty development offerings
are open to all faculty, regardless of status, at 63.75% of respondents' institutions, and an additional 8.75% of respondents offer some programs open
to adjunct faculty only. However, other data from our survey suggest that
adjunct faculty do not take advantage of these opportunities in numbers
proportional to their population. Adjuncts make up approximately half of all
faculty in the United States (Coalition on the Academic Workforce, 2012),
but when asked to estimate the percentage of participants accounted for
by adjunct faculty in their faculty development programs, 32.84% of item
respondents ($n = 67$) stated that adjunct faculty members account for fewer
than 10% of participants in their institutions' faculty development programs.
Adjuncts account for less than 40% of participants in faculty development
programs and services at 88.06% of item respondents' institutions. Possible
explanations for lower participation rates by adjunct faculty in professional
development include the inability of some centers to offer programming during evening hours and on weekends because of a lack of staff resources, a
reality noted by our respondents. In addition, adjunct faculty report that
they often are unaware they may participate in professional development or
assume such opportunities are only for full-time faculty. Anecdotal evidence
from developers also suggests that attracting participants takes time.

Respondents were asked whether their institution had an existing union
or union organizing activities. Only 46 of 80 survey respondents answered
this question, despite the fact that a "do not know" option was offered. This
unusual response pattern suggests that faculty developers may not have strong

connections to union activities on their campuses. Of those who answered the question, 30% indicated that their institution has an existing union for part-time faculty. Sixty-three of the 80 survey respondents answered the question "Are there adjunct-specific organizations on your campus?"; 33.33% of item respondents (26.25% of survey respondents) indicated that their institution has at least one adjunct-specific organization. The organizations identified by respondents include advisory committees or councils ($n = 6$), adjunct faculty associations ($n = 5$), an adjunct faculty learning community ($n = 1$), and an adjunct subcommittee of the faculty senate ($n = 1$).

When asked to identify one thing that their institution does well in support of adjunct faculty, seven respondents commented on an institutional culture that values adjunct and tenured faculty equally:

> [We treat] them as entirely equal faculty with respect to voting, access to institutional resources, expertise, etc.

Eight additional responses acknowledged the inclusion of adjunct faculty in the community as something their institution does particularly well. A total of 14 comments throughout the survey stated the importance of engaging adjunct faculty in the community of the institution:

> We work closely with HR to identify brand-new adjuncts and give them content and programming to help them feel "a part of" rather than "apart from" the institution.

On the other hand, many responses painted a troubling picture of the attitudes and treatment of adjuncts at their institution. Two respondents went so far as to say that their institution does not do anything well in support of adjunct faculty. Throughout the survey, 20 comments emphasized the limited institutional support provided to adjuncts:

> Seems to be little to no visible, impactful support from administration for these efforts.

> Departmental support varies widely but is generally low.

> We wish it were more important across the university than it really is.

Three responses noted the irony in the lack of support and opportunity for adjunct faculty members given that they make up a large percentage (often the majority) of faculty at their institution:

They represent sixty percent of our faculty. Why do we continue to ignore this group? They don't support them.

Throughout the survey, there were many comments tinged with resentment or other emotionally charged words or images. Some of the words and phrases that respondents used to describe their perception of the treatment of adjunct faculty include *disgraceful, crappy, ridiculous, replaceable, expendable, low regard, caste system,* and *second class.*

> Make them feel part of the university instead of second class citizens. It is disgraceful.

> It's a ridiculous system that hurts students and treats teachers like Kleenex: everyone is glad to have us when we're needed and happy to discard us when not.

Strategies for Adjunct Professional Development

As discussed in chapter 1, the working conditions faced by adjuncts often do not lend themselves to the provision of quality instruction, even if adjuncts are capable of and committed to teaching their students well. Four survey respondents noted this connection between a lack of adjunct support and a negative impact on students:

> Administrators pay lip service to students as priorities but they do not support adjunct faculty and therefore, shortchange both.

> [Adjunct faculty] need the tools to help our students be successful!

If institutions are going to employ adjunct faculty, they need to have structures in place to ensure that adjunct faculty are able to demonstrate excellence in their service to students and the rest of the institution. Our survey revealed a number of specific strategies and tips for supporting adjunct faculty, to the benefit of adjuncts, students, and other members of the institutional community.

Those surveyed were asked to describe one thing (program, service, etc.) that their institution or Center for Teaching and Learning did particularly well in support of adjunct faculty. The most common answers included the following:

- Communication about professional development opportunities and institutional expectations (*n* = 12)

- Adjunct orientation (n = 11)
- Inclusion of adjuncts in the majority of professional development offerings (n = 11)
- Providing incentives for adjuncts to participate in professional development (n = 8)
- Engaging adjuncts in the institutional community (n = 8)

When respondents were asked what one thing they would like to do to improve professional development for adjunct faculty at their institution, the most common response (n = 24) was to offer incentives for adjunct faculty to attend programs:

> We need to create job structures that incentivize, fund, and reward their participation in CTL activities. Full-time instructorships, long-term contracts, pay scales that reflect experience and development—all create mechanisms for encouraging faculty development activities.

Incentives are offered to adjunct faculty at 42.5% of respondents' institutions in order to boost participation in faculty development programs and services offered by the institution. Among these respondents whose institutions offer incentives for adjunct participation, 25.53% offer financial incentives paid to faculty. The rest offer incentives in other forms, including teaching certifications, letters of recommendation, and free parking.

Three respondents indicated that they would like to offer some form of recognition to adjunct faculty for participating in professional development or to show gratitude for exemplary teaching. Twelve respondents mentioned a specific program that they would like their institution to improve, expand, or add to their current offerings. Out of these, five would like to improve or offer an adjunct orientation, and two would like to see an adjunct mentoring program. Eleven respondents stated that they would like to conduct a needs assessment for adjunct faculty in order to develop more programming that responds to their specific needs.

An emphasis on intentionality is seen in the survey responses regarding what respondents' institutions are doing well and what they could be doing better, as well as in other comments throughout the survey. To be inclusive of adjuncts, faculty developers (and institutions as a whole) will need to be more intentional about how they welcome, involve, and support adjunct faculty. Fourteen responses noted that simply ensuring that adjunct faculty are invited to programs can make a difference in whether they feel welcome and whether they will attend. Although professional development offerings are open to adjunct faculty at many (if not most) institutions, adjuncts are often unaware of offerings or unsure whether programs and services are really "for them":

> We learned from some focus groups that it's important to explicitly state that adjunct faculty are included in the invitation for events or services. Otherwise, they may think they're not even though they are.

Another way to be intentional in supporting adjunct faculty is to make programs and services more accessible by either adjusting or expanding the hours of offerings ($n = 7$) or offering programs and services in an online format ($n = 9$):

> [We] offer workshops at various times to meet adjunct schedules.

> [We] offer online faculty development programs to allow for anytime/ anywhere participation.

Respondents also recommended that institutions be more intentional about serving adjunct faculty by attempting to understand their specific needs and respond to those needs through advocacy or programming designed especially for them:

> [We should create] a position in our center dedicated to identifying needs of adjunct faculty who could advocate for and help develop stronger sup- port structures, better policies for working conditions, and (as appropriate) professional development.

> We program with them in mind and strive to have them feel welcomed to all of our programming.

Programming designed to meet the specific needs of adjunct faculty is offered at 66.25% of respondents' institutions. Common programs offered specifically for adjunct faculty include orientation sessions (offered by 53.75% of respondents' institutions), single sessions on specific teaching and learning topics (36.25%), classroom technology training (23.75%), class- room observation (22.5%), and faculty learning communities (21.25%). Respondents representing public colleges were more likely to report that their institutions developed programs specifically for adjunct faculty. This difference was found to be statistically significant.

Finally, a few respondents contended that the best way institutions can support part-time faculty is by getting them into a full-time position ($n = 4$):

Open paths to full-time employment.

It is important to note that a strategy that was helpful in supporting adjunct faculty at one institution may not be beneficial or feasible at another. Some respondents noted that a strategy that was largely applauded by our respondents as a whole did not work for them:

> We used to develop programs specifically targeted at PT [part-time] faculty and found that over the years, this wasn't working and they didn't appreciate being singled out.

> [We] tried offering extended hours at the CTL [Center for Teaching and Learning] for adjunct faculty specifically, but not enough adjunct faculty took advantage of it to justify cost.

Challenges in Supporting Adjunct Faculty

When asked what they felt were the most significant challenges in supporting adjunct faculty, nearly half of respondents noted that time and availability were major issues ($n = 39$):

> TIME. Both in expecting them to give time when they're not compensated, but also working around their schedules for those not available during the day.

Another challenge identified by respondents was limited resources, primarily in terms of funding to incentivize professional development or provide better pay and benefits ($n = 18$) as well as in terms of limited personnel resources for offering services and programs at times when adjunct faculty can access them ($n = 4$).

Respondents also said the working conditions faced by adjunct faculty could pose challenges for involving them in professional development. Last-minute hiring ($n = 3$), a sense of isolation ($n = 3$), job instability ($n = 2$), low compensation ($n = 3$), and a lack of access to resources such as curriculum maps ($n = 1$) were all listed as challenges in supporting adjunct faculty:

> [The] main challenge is retaining employment and making a living on low compensation in unstable jobs, given the system of semester by semester, course by course employment, and then somehow building upon that unstable foundation to be productive, creative, and advancing scholars with minimal support.

> [A challenge is] supporting innovation—adjunct faculty have less leeway and face higher risk in trying new things.

The most frequently mentioned challenge related to adjunct working conditions was the nature of adjunct contracts ($n = 9$). Some respondents stated that adjunct faculty members' tendency to be transient might have an effect on their commitment to the institution or their sense of belonging:

> It's hard to get to a sense of belonging when they're patching together lives from various institutions.

> They're often only staying until a tenure-track job comes along, so they may not be as invested in the institution as full-time faculty.

The fact that many adjunct faculty are at an institution for only a short period (and the real or perceived effect this may have on their level of commitment) may be at odds with departmental or institutional investment in them. Institutions may feel that they cannot afford to invest resources in faculty that might not be there next semester:

> Many are long-term adjuncts, but some are in and out in short, unpredictable time frames. That makes it difficult to justify to administration expenditures of support (stipends and time) for adjuncts who may or may not be (or become) established members of the campus community.

As noted previously, intentionally inviting adjunct faculty to professional development offerings can go a long way in increasing participation and making them feel welcome. However, many respondents throughout the survey noted the challenge of identifying and getting in touch with adjunct faculty given the nature of their temporary or at-will employment:

> One key challenge for us, even when our center wants to enhance adjunct-only offerings, is finding an appropriate way to reach them! Institutional [electronic mailing lists] have been notoriously unreliable.

> [We need to] have them gain their access to our systems earlier so we could be in touch with them earlier.

Finally, seven respondents mentioned challenges based on the varied nature of adjunct faculty's needs and situations:

[A challenge is] addressing diverse needs of adjuncts who are often located in a variety of locations/cities.

Scheduling times and opportunities that work for the varied needs of our adjunct community.

Conclusion

Although not representative of faculty developers across the nation, our survey findings offer insight into the current state of adjunct faculty development and the possibilities for improvement therein. On one hand, we've seen evidence of institutional cultures that support their adjunct faculty, demonstrate concern for their well-being, and/or actively seek to include them in the broader faculty community. On the other hand, many survey responses reveal the overall lack of support for adjunct faculty on many campuses and hint at the psychological burden placed on them as a result of being excluded and perceived as inferior members of the academy. Several respondents indicated that their institution is just beginning to recognize and respond to challenges faced by adjunct faculty:

We have turned things around from having no care for our adjuncts several years ago to where the adjuncts are now talking about how great a job we do.

We are making it a goal this year to improve services to and participation from adjunct faculty.

This may point toward a shift in attitudes in the field of higher education about the importance of supporting adjunct faculty. Still, there are many financial, structural, and cultural challenges we have yet to overcome. Even where professional development and support are offered to adjunct faculty, systematic barriers and the nature of their positions can inhibit adjunct faculty members from taking advantage of provided opportunities.

Major areas of growth for supporting adjunct faculty include giving them a voice in institutional governance and increasing their sense of belonging in the community. These themes were reiterated by the stories of adjunct faculty members in part one of this book. Smaller steps that institutions might take to improve adjunct support were also identified, such as improving communication about professional development opportunities and assessing the varied needs of the institution's adjunct population in order to develop relevant programs and services. The benefits of improving the level of adjunct support in higher education extends beyond adjunct faculty members to the students they teach and to the institution as a whole. By establishing a culture of support for adjunct faculty, institutions can demonstrate both their appreciation for adjunct educators and their commitment to student learning.

References

Coalition on the Academic Workforce. (2012). *A portrait of part-time faculty members: A summary of findings on part-time faculty respondents to the Coalition on the Academic Workforce survey of contingent faculty members and instructors.* Retrieved from http://www.academicworkforce.org/CAW_portrait_2012.pdf

Sorcinelli, M. D., Austin, A. E., Eddy, P. L., & Beach, A. L. (2006). *Creating the future of faculty development: Learning from the past, understanding the present.* San Francisco, CA: Anker.

8

Model Programs Across the Country

Roy Fuller

W hen we developed our call for chapter submissions for this book, we thought we would receive stories from adjunct faculty who had found and benefited from professional development opportunities. We also hoped we would hear from individuals who had found community, whether of their own making or through the institutions they serve. We received both types of submissions, and they are featured in part one. To our delight, a number of submissions described existing formalized professional development opportunities for adjunct faculty, and we felt that they warranted inclusion as a separate part. The selections in part two focus less on the unique personal experiences of adjunct faculty and more on the types of services, programs, and recognition efforts that are vitally important to supporting adjunct faculty in their teaching. Contributors describe a wide range of programs that demonstrate creativity in both outreach and recognition of adjunct faculty. Our hope is that adjunct and full-time faculty, department chairs, course coordinators, administrators, and faculty developers will find both inspiration and concrete strategies they can seek to implement on their own campuses.

As has been noted previously, the training and development needs of adjunct faculty related to teaching and instructional design are, in many ways, no different from the needs of tenure-track, or non-tenure-track, full-time faculty. To achieve their full potential, all educators can benefit from ongoing guidance in pedagogy, educational technology, course design, assessment and evaluation, and the many other offerings typically provided by Centers for Teaching and Learning and professional organizations. One of our purposes in *Adjunct Faculty Voices* is to describe the unique challenges of serving this growing and highly transient segment of the academic workforce. Respondents of our survey revealed the challenges and rewards of supporting adjunct faculty with programs designed with their unique needs in mind. The selections featured in this chapter include descriptions of comprehensive, large-scale programs as well as smaller offerings and demonstrate the

87

positive impact that both can have. We understand that financial and staffing resources are tight on many campuses, so we want to provide a variety of examples for how campus leaders can support their adjunct faculty.

The first three selections in part two describe "full-service" programs, interconnected and integrated support services for adjunct faculty. In their appropriately titled chapter "Creating Faculty Development Opportunities for Adjuncts," Suzanne Tapp and Andrea McCourt reveal a wide range of strategies and programs to stimulate adjunct participation in professional development. Tapp and McCourt remind us that simply stating that adjunct faculty are welcome to participate in a center's or university's professional development programs is not sufficient. Beginning with orientation sessions that include practical information about the institution, department, and learning management system (LMS), the Teaching, Learning, and Professional Development Center at Texas Tech University provides support to adjunct faculty engaged in both face-to-face and online teaching environments. Tapp and McCourt discuss mentor programs, advocacy for adjunct faculty, and the promotion of adjunct faculty in institutional governance as key approaches to support the adjunct community they serve.

Advocacy has become increasingly significant for faculty developers seeking to support adjunct faculty. In his chapter about adjunct professional development at Kirkwood Community College (KCC), Larry Bonde describes how a college or university might come to not only understand the needs of adjunct faculty but also involve adjunct faculty in their own advocacy. Toward this end, KCC deploys an annual survey to gather demographic information and feedback about communication preferences, instructional resources, and climate issues. These data are used to inform the work of the Adjunct Faculty Advisory Committee (AFAC), which for over 20 years has served as the voice of the adjunct community. This group sets annual goals to assess its progress in supporting adjunct faculty. KCC also supports an annual Adjunct Service Recognition event that is hosted by the college president. In addition, the AFAC Professional Development Fund was established to encourage adjunct faculty to continue their development through conferences, workshops, and graduate courses.

Although the phrases "adjunct faculty" and "scholarly teaching" are rarely seen together, Saginaw Valley State University (SVSU) offers a model of adjunct development based on the Lyons and Burnstad (2007) best practices model that strives to promote scholarly teachers. In their chapter, Ann Coburn-Collins, Anne M. Acker, Lester L. Altevogt, and Lisa S. Tsay describe a peer-mentoring program, a professional development funding program, and their use of adjunct faculty learning communities. To reach more adjunct faculty, and in acknowledgment of the challenges involved in scheduling, SVSU launched an online orientation. Many survey respondents noted that compensating adjunct faculty for their time and participation is important and something they wished they could offer. SVSU provides a model program that compensates adjunct faculty who participate in workshops, orientations, mentor programs, and conferences.

The next chapter features a single program at GateWay Community College. Contributors Summer Cherland, Heather Crook, Lindsay Dippold, J.W. Gaberdiel, and Jenalee Remy were among the inaugural participants in an "Excellence in Teaching" Adjunct Faculty Academy (AFA). In their chapter, they describe the program goals, how it was developed and launched, and how the participants applied the lessons learned in their teaching. Although community building is not explicitly identified as an objective of the AFA, the experience of community described by the authors is notable and reiterates the value of collegial support.

The final chapter, written by Ruth Fagan, reveals how one school at a Research I institution uses an adjunct liaison to support the growing numbers of adjunct faculty who are employed by the school. The adjunct liaison position provides a vital link between adjunct faculty and full-time faculty and advocates for adjunct faculty needs to administrators. Fagan notes that student feedback has revealed no statistical difference between the overall quality of classroom instruction received from tenured and tenure-track faculty and that from adjunct instructors. As the debate about the impact of adjunct faculty on student learning rages, Fagan's piece demonstrates how the effective use of an adjunct liaison can contribute not only to better trained adjunct faculty but also to student success.

We hope that you gather from our contributors a wealth of ideas, examples, and strategies—both comprehensive and program based—for consideration and implementation to support adjunct faculty members within your own institutional context.

Reference

Lyons, R. E., & Burnstad, H. (2007). *Best practices for supporting adjunct faculty.* Paper presented at the Chair Academy's Annual Conference, Jacksonville, FL.

9

Creating Faculty Development Opportunities for Adjuncts

Suzanne Tapp and Andrea McCourt

In recent years, adjunct faculty have played an increasingly prominent role in higher education. With over half of all collegiate instruction being provided by adjunct faculty (U.S. Department of Education, 2010), it seems imperative to support adjunct faculty in their teaching endeavors. Much of the current dialogue about adjuncts addresses topics such as the advantages and disadvantages of using adjuncts or contingent faculty (Flaherty, 2014; McCarthy, 2014) or focuses on issues related to adjunct compensation and benefits (Lewin, 2013). It also seems important to investigate the availability and effectiveness of professional development opportunities offered to adjunct faculty. With our own experience as the executive director of the Teaching, Learning, and Professional Development Center and the program director of the Human Resource Development Undergraduate Program, respectively, and as adjuncts at multiple institutions, we are uniquely situated to provide personal insight and lessons learned about experiencing and designing professional development opportunities for adjuncts. From this vantage point, we have written specifically for faculty developers, chairs, and administrators who seek practical ideas and examples to best support their adjunct faculty members.

In their 2013 study, Mueller, Mandernach, and Sanderson found that overall student learning and course satisfaction were lower in classes taught by adjunct faculty than in those taught by full-time faculty. They suggested that this gap does not indicate that adjunct faculty are less effective teachers. Rather, the explanation comes from the fact that the vast majority of faculty training and development opportunities are geared for tenure-track faculty. This problem is often exacerbated by the fact that adjunct faculty frequently feel isolated from other faculty and the larger campus community (Dobbins, 2011). Blodgett (2008) reported that many adjunct faculty members express a desire to engage in teaching and professional development opportunities.

However, those types of opportunities are not always available to adjunct faculty. Even when such opportunities are available, adjunct faculty seldom receive the same incentives or financial support to attend these events, and they are unlikely to receive support for conference attendance.

At our home institution, Texas Tech University, the Teaching, Learning, and Professional Development Center (TLPDC) serves as the hub for faculty development events from a broad, campus-level approach. The TLPDC offers teaching and learning workshops ranging from foundation-level topics such as syllabus development and classroom management to specific pedagogy-oriented sessions that focus on topics such as mindfulness in the classroom and service-learning. After nearly two decades, the philosophy of the center's leadership remains the same: All are welcome to attend any event offered through the TLPDC, including staff, graduate student instructors, and faculty of all ranks. Adjunct faculty members are welcome at these events and receive invitations via campus mail and e-mail. But does offering a blanket welcome mean that adjunct faculty members will join professional development opportunities and find a place to make their voices heard? As one might expect, our experience shows that some adjuncts will participate and some will feel excluded regardless, and therefore, we feel that it is our obligation to pursue adjuncts in several specific ways. Purposed steps are taken to help ensure that adjunct faculty have the opportunity to interact with other campus faculty members and that they are aware of the variety of professional development opportunities that are available to them on campus. We want to make sure that adjunct faculty feel welcome and know that the university supports their teaching efforts.

The TLPDC coordinates New Faculty Orientation and works with departments to identify new tenure-track faculty, visiting professors, and adjunct faculty members or, as they are called on our campus, professors of practice. Although they are not required to attend, they are invited, and we have found that coordinating an opportunity for adjuncts to have lunch with their deans and chairs on the day of New Faculty Orientation has proved to be an important introductory opportunity for all involved that otherwise might not occur. Promoting this lunch opportunity often garners the participation of adjuncts, but we have also found that adjuncts are typically in survival mode when they enter our university system. In some departments, they are given a thorough introduction to university resources such as Blackboard access and parking, but in others, they are simply left to discover these resources themselves. Because we offer them this information, our practical help serves as a welcome mat and helps us establish a relationship with adjuncts that often results in their participation in other professional development offerings. For example, several professors of practice or adjuncts have participated in our Service-Learning Faculty Fellowship Program in which they receive a stipend and a graduate assistant to help them establish a service-learning-designated course.

One way to gain participation from adjuncts comes from selecting topics for professional development in which they might have interest. For example, on our campus, our highest attendance numbers from adjuncts come from sessions oriented around teaching online. This experience taught us that providing workshops that correlate with the specific concerns or interests of adjunct faculty helps increase their participation in professional development opportunities. Another extremely helpful way to encourage adjunct participation in professional development opportunities is to use terms such as *adjunct faculty* or *instructors* in workshop titles or descriptions to make these individuals aware that the workshops are relevant for them and that they are welcome at the event. In addition, as we have sought ways to both give adjuncts a voice and get them involved in professional development, we found that hosting a roundtable forum with our senior vice provost and asking adjuncts to share their pressing needs was by far the best outreach we have had. This strategy is a win-win for both groups (administration and adjuncts) and has gone far in making tangible changes such as the career ladder now resulting from the professor of practice rank.

Although providing access to New Faculty Orientation and professional development opportunities is certainly beneficial, it does not address all of the needs of adjunct faculty. Many adjunct and contingent faculty members report that they frequently receive teaching assignments a few weeks or even a few days before the start of the semester and are provided little to no training related to campus teaching expectations, access to departmental resources such as photocopiers, or even information on how to use required technology such as online learning management systems (LMSs) (Meixner, Kruck, & Madden, 2010). Some adjunct faculty members are simply given the location of their class and a copy of the textbook. Perhaps they are also given a copy of an old syllabus for extra help. This sets up a "sink or swim" type of experience, and this lack of training and operational information can make it extremely difficult for adjunct faculty members to perform their job duties. There are several practices that we feel are especially effective in welcoming adjunct faculty to the institution and training them how to be effective in their job from day one.

"Pretraining" programs can be especially effective for adjunct faculty members. Although campus-level faculty orientation programs such as the one at our home institution are extremely helpful, they do not always help new faculty understand how to function in their departments or how to get simple, practical things (e.g., unlocking the door to a classroom, knowing what to include in a syllabus, etc.) accomplished. New Faculty Orientation frequently covers HR-related topics such as information about compensation and benefits, followed by the opportunity to fill out the necessary paperwork. Providing these opportunities for adjunct faculty indicates that they are important to the institution. Berry (2005) argued that faculty should be paid for attending orientation activities. Berry went on to state that paying for the adjuncts' time shows that the institution sees their time as a valuable resource. Indeed, some institutions pay a $500 stipend for attending New Faculty Orientation and/or completing requisite training (e.g., how to use the university's online LMS). It may be helpful to offer orientations at the start of each teaching semester or term, as adjuncts are hired throughout the year. These orientations can be offered on campus and through virtual meeting platforms such as Lync or Skype. It can also be very effective to offer asynchronous orientations in an online LMS such as Blackboard or Desire2Learn. Specifically, we recommend that adjunct training should address topics such as (a) departmental policies and procedures, (b) a list of departmental or campus resources for faculty, (c) a clear reporting structure for adjunct faculty so that they know who to contact with questions or concerns, (d) information about relevant technology for the classroom, (e) procedural information such as how and when to submit grades or assessment results, and (f) a list of expectations for adjunct faculty.

Given the growth in online learning and the fact that many institutions hire adjuncts to teach online courses, we feel that it is important to address the unique training needs of online adjunct faculty. Online teaching requires unique pedagogical skills and specific training. Research (Ray, 2009; Terantino & Agbehonou, 2012) has indicated that faculty members feel that both technical and pedagogical training related to online teaching is desirable and helpful. Most campuses have an LMS such as Blackboard or Desire2Learn for the majority of online courses, and even experienced online faculty can benefit from training on how to use the campus LMS. We strongly recommend that this training be provided before the semester begins so new faculty know how to access their class and begin teaching from day one of the semester. We also recommend that online faculty (especially new faculty) be given early access to training on online teaching skills and strategies as well. On our campus, we have more than 50 face-to-face training sessions available throughout the year specific to our LMS, but we also recorded many of these sessions, as we realized that many of our faculty, especially the adjunct members, were not as likely to attend these sessions. The convenience of online training coupled with instructional design consultation via Skype or Lync has proved to be a winning combination for adjuncts and an efficient use of staff resources for our eLearning program.

Given the transient nature of adjunct employment at different institutions or departments and the limited amount of time adjuncts have to prepare for a course, it is easy to see how they can feel uninformed regarding operating policies and other important aspects of teaching at different institutions (e.g., how to handle grade appeals, how to access campus resources such as a testing center, etc.). This problem is exacerbated by the fact that many adjunct faculty avoid asking too many questions because they do not want to appear inept for fear of jeopardizing future teaching assignments. We have observed a "stay under the radar" mentality many adjuncts may adopt instead of handling student confrontations, questioning course design problems, giving feedback about curriculum decisions, or even communicating about their own needs if they need a break from teaching for a semester for personal reasons. This can lead to a dangerous pattern of uninformed decision-making; unempowered teaching decisions; and, ultimately, burned-out adjunct faculty members. It seems plausible that some adjunct faculty members use this "under the radar" approach because they do not want to lose future teaching opportunities. Colleges and universities compound this problem by offering adjunct teaching contracts one semester at a time, which sends a message that employment is temporary. When teaching contracts are offered at the last minute, this can make employment feel even more nebulous to adjunct faculty members. Institutions could send a much stronger message that adjuncts are valued and that their unique skills are desirable by offering contracts ahead of time. Some schools offer fall and spring contracts at the same time, which is appreciated by most contingent faculty. Adding a statement that "employment is dependent on adequate enrollment" makes this a low-risk enterprise.

Last-minute teaching offers can also lead to the unintended outcome of overloaded adjunct faculty. Many contingent faculty teach at more than one institution. In keeping with their desire to please and to secure steady employment, some adjunct faculty members feel compelled to accept any and all teaching offers. This can mean that adjunct faculty members take on too much, and their teaching may suffer as a result. Adjuncts may also accept class offerings that aren't a good match with their expertise for the same reason—to stay in a department head's good graces. This can also have negative impacts on teaching. Everyone benefits when department heads or faculty schedulers plan ahead and carefully match faculty to appropriate classes. Advance planning and staffing leads to happier, better prepared adjunct faculty and thus better learning for the students.

Another highly regarded solution to support adjuncts can be found in faculty mentoring programs. Faculty mentoring programs are an excellent way to help new faculty members feel welcome and competent (Beans, 1999;

Luna & Cullen, 1995). Some institutions require all first-semester adjunct faculty members to have a faculty mentor, who may be selected from the ranks of the senior adjunct faculty members with a great track record in the department. These faculty mentors are frequently compensated a small amount (around $500) for serving as a mentor. These mentors can help the new adjuncts in a variety of ways, including providing information about policies or procedures, making suggestions on how to handle situations, giving advice on campus and departmental politics, and so on.

As we noted earlier, many adjunct faculty members report a feeling of isolation from other campus (especially tenure-track) faculty. Many others have expressed frustration at their lack of voice at their institutions. One excellent remedy to these issues is to involve adjunct faculty in shared governance. Indeed, the American Association of University Professors (AAUP) recently recommended that adjunct faculty members be given full membership and voting status in institutional governance bodies such as the faculty senate (Basu, 2012). This recognition in shared governance is an important and public statement that adjunct faculty and their opinions are important. Involvement in shared governance bodies can increase adjunct faculty members' feelings of inclusion, and their voices can make valuable contributions to institutional teaching and learning. Given the large number of adjunct faculty on college campuses and the significant percentage of classes taught by these adjunct faculty, it seems important for institutions to hear more about their experiences, opinions, and needs. When adjunct faculty have a venue to voice their opinions, the faculty members certainly feel more involved and appreciated, which is valuable. Again, we refer to the roundtable event hosted by the provost's office with adjunct faculty as an excellent example of such a venue. The TLPDC also includes an adjunct faculty member on the center's Advisory Committee and seeks specific feedback regarding programming as we strive to meet the professional development needs of adjuncts. The fact that institutions gain information about how to improve adjunct faculty members' work, which then helps them teach students more effectively, is an added bonus.

Administrators at all levels can do many things to help adjuncts feel like a valued part of the faculty and to serve as an advocate for adjuncts. Providing reasonable pay and access to benefits (whether this means health care benefits or even more limited benefits such as free or paid access to professional development opportunities) can go a long way to show that an institution is invested in the long-term employment and success of an adjunct. Pay raises based on longevity are another way to show that the institution desires a long-term professional relationship with contingent faculty. Providing access to things such as physical office space, software, photocopiers, and help from departmental support staff is also beneficial. Colleges and universities provide many resources to tenure-track faculty, including travel grants, tuition reimbursement, and fellowship programs. Extending these opportunities to adjunct faculty as well sends a strong message that adjunct faculty are valued and that the institution is willing to invest in their success.

In our experience, professional development leaders and administrators may lack audience awareness in regard to adjuncts and typically might overlook their big picture issues such as an overwhelming course load, unsatisfactory compensation, time management challenges, and lack of professional development funding available. We see ourselves at a distinct advantage as we both hold administrative appointments *and* adjunct roles on our campus. To help others gain a broader awareness and sense of audience, we take small steps such as making our presenters aware of registered attendees prior to events and helping them note the range of attendees, whether they are tenure track, tenured, adjunct, or staff. At the very least, promoting audience awareness and acting as advocates for adjuncts can only contribute to a broader understanding of the roles that others on campus play, aside from traditional tenure-track faculty. Investing in adjunct faculty members' professional development, supporting them in the classroom, and including their voice on campus positively affects their job performance and satisfaction. We believe the ideas outlined in this chapter can help institutions develop more effective adjunct faculty and provide stronger learning experiences for their students. By taking these steps, institutions can truly maximize the potential of adjunct faculty and support both the traditional tenure-track faculty and the newer and quickly growing group of adjuncts to promote high-quality learning experiences for all of their students.

References

Basu, K. (2012, June 28). Voting rights for adjuncts. *Inside Higher Ed*. Retrieved from https://www.insidehighered.com/news/2012/06/28/aaup-report-stresses-need-adjunct-involvement-governance

Beans, B. E. (1999). Mentoring program helps young faculty feel at home. *APA Monitor Online, 30*(3).

Berry, J. (2005). *Reclaiming the ivory tower: Organizing adjuncts to change higher education*. New York, NY: Monthly Review.

Blodgett, M. C. (2008). *Adjunct faculty perceptions of needs in preparation to teach online* (Doctoral dissertation, Capella University). Retrieved from http://search.proquest.com/pqdtglobal/docview/304816589

Dobbins, K. (2011). Reflections on SoTL by a casual lecturer: Personal benefits, long-term challenges. *International Journal for the Scholarship of Teaching and*

Learning, 5(2). Retrieved from http://digitalcommons.georgiasouthern.edu/cgi/viewcontent.cgi?article=1309&context=ij-sotl

Flaherty, C. (2014, January 24). Congress takes note. *Inside Higher Ed.* Retrieved from https://www.insidehighered.com/news/2014/01/24/house-committee-report-highlights-plight-adjunct-professors

Lewin, T. (2013, December 3). More college adjuncts see strengths in union numbers. *The New York Times.* Retrieved from http://www.nytimes.com/2013/12/04/us/more-college-adjuncts-see-strength-in-union-numbers.html?_r=0

Luna, G., & Cullen, D. (1995). *Empowering the faculty: Mentoring redirected and renewed* (ASHE-ERIC Higher Education Report No. 3). Retrieved from http://files.eric.ed.gov/fulltext/ED399889.pdf

McCarthy, C. (2014, August 22). Adjunct professors fight for crumbs on campus. *The Washington Post.* Retrieved from http://wpo.st/RY4X1

Meixner, C., Kruck, S. E., & Madden, L. T. (2010). Inclusion of part-time faculty for the benefit of faculty and students. *College Teaching, 58*(4), 141–147. doi:10.1080/87567555.20 10.484032

Mueller, B., Mandernach, B. J., & Sanderson, K. (2013). Adjunct versus full-time faculty: Comparison of student outcomes in online education. *Journal of Online Learning and Teaching, 9*(3). Retrieved from http://jolt.merlot.org/vol9no3/mueller_0913.htm

Ray, J. (2009). Faculty perspective: Training and development for the online classroom. *MERLOT Journal of Online Learning and Teaching, 5*(2), 263–276. Retrieved from http://jolt.merlot.org/vol5no2/ray_0609.pdf

Terantino, J. M., & Agbehonou, E. (2012). Comparing faculty perceptions of an online development course: Addressing faculty needs for online teaching. *Online Journal of Distance Learning Administration, 15*(2). Retrieved from http://www.westga.edu/~distance/ojdla/summer152/terantino_agbehonou152.html

U.S. Department of Education. (2010). *The condition of education 2010.* Washington, DC: National Center for Educational Statistics, Institute of Educational Sciences. Retrieved from https://nces.ed.gov/pubs2010/2010028.pdf

10

Creating an Adjunct Community and Supporting Its Professional Development

Kirkwood Community College

Larry Bonde

K irkwood Community College (Kirkwood) has a proactive approach to the support of the members of its adjunct community and their professional development. Kirkwood has long considered adjuncts a valued part of its faculty. The adjuncts provide an economic and flexible component to Kirkwood's teaching personnel and on average provide 40% of the credit hours taught and 60% of the instructional staff. As such Kirkwood is continually working to deliver a wide-ranging system of supports that integrates adjuncts into the Kirkwood faculty community and aids them in developing their professional skills or advancing their careers.

About Kirkwood Community College and Its Adjunct Population

Kirkwood, an institute of higher learning in eastern Iowa, was founded in 1966. The college serves a seven-county area with people from all walks of life. Kirkwood has students attending from all 99 counties within Iowa, as well as 32 states and 100 countries. The mission of the college is to identify community needs; provide accessible, quality education and training; and promote opportunities for lifelong learning.

The Kirkwood adjunct community includes any instructor who has taught credit hours in the past academic year. Normally there are 800 instructors of whom 550 teach in the fall and spring semesters. Like any community, it is a diverse group with a variety of interests and levels of involvement. Based on the 284 responses to the November 2014 annual adjunct survey, which represent about 35% of the active adjunct instructors, the demographics of the adjunct community are as follows: The average age is 51.2 years, 92.3% are Caucasians, 59.4% are females, 88% have master's degrees or higher, the average number of years teaching at Kirkwood is 5.7 years, and the average number of credit hours taught per academic year is 8.5 hours. The career interests of the community varied among aspiring full-timers (35%), career enders (19%), specialists (28%), freelancers (12%), and Kirkwood staff (5%).

The Adjunct Faculty Advisory Committee

The adjunct community has evolved over the years because of the efforts of the Adjunct Faculty Advisory Committee (AFAC) and administration. AFAC was formed in 1994 when a group of adjuncts approached Kirkwood administration with a proposal to establish a committee to be the "voice of the adjunct community." The proposal was accepted. Over the years it has grown into an organized and effective representation of the adjunct faculty, enhancing the integration of adjuncts in the Kirkwood faculty community.

AFAC normally consists of 12 adjunct volunteers and 7 college administrators. The executive board is made up of an administrative cochair, adjunct cochair, vice cochair, secretary, and communication director. All officer positions are elected by members of AFAC for a one-year term. Typically, there are one or more adjunct representatives from each department and regional center. The administrative representatives consist of two deans, three directors, one human resources director, and staff from Kirkwood's Center for Excellence in Learning and Teaching (KCELT).

The AFAC group meets monthly in the fall and spring semesters. It operates from a documented manual and operating procedure. Over the summer, the AFAC executive committee meets twice for planning purposes. Guided by the annual survey, the executive committee sets annual measurable goals that are used to form meeting agendas. Those annual goals will vary but often focus on participation levels in a variety of social and educational events; use of development funds; improvement in process and procedural areas; faculty integration; and onboarding, orientation, and mentoring. AFAC has subcommittees for each goal and other ongoing activities. Committees and groups work on activities between meetings and report progress at the monthly meetings. Only the adjunct representatives have voting privileges; administrative members provide input and support. Selected members of AFAC meet three times a year to discuss policy and practice matters and meet annually with the vice president of academic affairs to review activities and opportunities from the past year. AFAC presents a progress report to the Kirkwood board of trustees biannually.

Kirkwood's adjuncts have formed a community through the efforts of AFAC with the support of the Kirkwood administration. AFAC has done this by taking the time to understand adjuncts' needs and working with administration to improve policies and procedures relative to adjunct professional development and to include adjuncts in Kirkwood and departmental communications, meetings, and social activities.

Understanding the Adjuncts: The Annual Adjunct Survey

The Kirkwood adjuncts are a diverse group of individuals with varying backgrounds and interests in being integrated into the Kirkwood faculty, from those who aspire to be full-time employees and want to be involved in the community to those who just want to teach and not be involved any further. Because of the varied nature of adjunct faculty work, the initial step in supporting adjuncts is gaining an understanding of their needs and concerns. To that end, every fall AFAC e-mails a web survey to the approximately 800 active adjuncts. Survey administration is coordinated with the assistance of Kirkwood's Department of Institutional Research. The normal response rate is 35%. There are approximately 50 questions, which focus on demographics, opinions on college resources, communication, staff interactions, and other topics.

Survey results are compiled, analyzed, and reported by AFAC. The survey data are graphed in aggregate as well as for individual departments. They are plotted over time to show trends and indicate areas where additional focus should be considered. A report is made available to the adjunct community and to academic affairs and all departmental deans. The results are also used for the report made by AFAC to the board of trustees every two years. This survey has been used to help AFAC and administration set goals and formulate action plans to address the concerns of Kirkwood's adjunct population. The goals cover a variety of items such as use of professional development funds, increasing event attendance, and improvement of Kirkwood resources. The impacts of the actions taken are then evaluated in forthcoming surveys to determine results.

Getting off to a Good Start: Orientation of New Adjunct Hires

The results of the 2014 survey revealed a need to further improve the process of onboarding, orienting, and mentoring new adjuncts. To that end,

Kirkwood administration and KCELT worked with AFAC to develop and implement a more formal, standardized orientation process. The goal is to provide new adjuncts a positive and rapid integration into the Kirkwood family and to encourage retention.

The onboarding process includes a standard new hire checklist for all newly hired instructors. Items covered on the list include the Kirkwood faculty handbook, department policies and procedures, evaluation processes, job benefits, college communication, and key college contacts. The hiring department will then meet with the new adjunct to answer questions and talk in detail about college and department crucial items. An "Advantages and Benefits" document is also being created to share with new adjuncts to ensure they are aware of Kirkwood benefits. The departments send just-in-time reminders with further instructions on completing certain tasks, such as grading. In addition, adjuncts are assigned a mentor who is either full-time or a seasoned adjunct in the area they are teaching. This mentor is also another resource who is available to help as needed.

New adjuncts are also encouraged to participate in adjunct-specific orientation courses offered by KCELT. "Jumpstart" is the first course that would be recommended to all new adjuncts in their first semester. The Jumpstart course is a 90-minute orientation course designed to give new adjuncts the fundamental tools and training they need to get started. The course explores basic classroom teaching strategies and covers items such as where to locate the college syllabus template, what items should be included in the syllabus, how to use the learning management system (LMS), how to access e-mail, and how to navigate to the Kirkwood Information Network (KIN) SharePoint site. In addition to Jumpstart, Kirkwood offers a more in-depth adjunct orientation course online. Adjuncts can take this course before, during, or after their first semester. This 16-week online session explores learner-centered teaching strategies in the classroom and how to use effective learning assessments and engage in self-reflection. The successful completion includes a final project based on the participants' pedagogical interests. In a typical semester, 25% of Kirkwood's 25 to 30 new adjuncts will take advantage of the KCELT courses, and 70% of those will complete them.

Ongoing Support: Professional Development for Adjuncts

Support for adjuncts does not end after orientation. Kirkwood offers a number of professional development programs to provide for ongoing skill building. A variety of free events and activities offered through KCELT are available to help adjuncts develop their teaching skills. These activities may take the form of institutes, initiatives, individual sessions, or online courses. For example, KCELT hosts a variety of different "Best Practices" sessions. Adjuncts may take one or all of the sessions and receive a $50 stipend for each 90-minute session they attend. In fall 2015, these sessions included the following topics: active learning aims and practices, best practices for adjunct faculty, building classroom community, and outcomes and assessments. The Faculty Development Fellows program is another excellent teaching support opportunity for adjuncts. Participation as a faculty fellow is achieved through an application process and rewarded with a monetary stipend. Accepted fellows work on specific projects that are focused on improving student learning and teaching.

Adjunct faculty can connect with KCELT to have one-on-one consultations with the KCELT instructional design team to address particular challenges they may be facing in their class and to collaborate on finding solutions or improvements. Adjuncts might also take advantage of KCELT's Curriculum Design Support for guidance in aligning learning outcomes, assessment methods, and teaching and learning activities.

Also in support of teaching and learning is the annual Kirkwood AFAC state educational conference. With the support of Kirkwood administration, AFAC hosts a one-day conference featuring keynote speakers, student panels, workshops, and roundtable discussions. The conference focuses on new technology, classroom techniques, and other items of teaching and learning interest.

Professional development opportunities available to Kirkwood adjunct faculty extend beyond teaching and learning support. To assist adjuncts in furthering their career, AFAC hosts an annual roundtable event for adjuncts interested in full-time employment as an instructor or other educator. The roundtable consists of a group of deans, an HR representative, and past adjuncts who have been hired to full-time faculty and dean positions. These full-time professional educators present their perspective on the process for those hoping to be selected for full-time employment. The event is streamed live for those who wish to participate remotely. A video is stored for later review on the AFAC website. The information from this annual event is added to the "Adjunct to Full-Time" guidelines that are posted on the AFAC website.

Adjuncts are encouraged by administration to continue their academic interests through conferences, workshops, and graduate courses. To support these endeavors, the college allocates funding for academic professional development. Adjunct faculty are eligible for up to $550 per year in professional development funding. An application process through the dean of the academic department and the vice president of academic affairs is required for requesting funds. In addition, adjuncts may take two free academic classes each year to pursue academic or personal interests.

Full Integration With the Campus Community

Kirkwood takes a number of additional steps to improve integration of adjuncts and create a sense of belonging at the college—both major AFAC goals derived from the adjunct survey results. Communication with adjuncts has been improved communications to adjuncts. Through annual survey data, AFAC learned that Kirkwood adjuncts prefer to have information provided to them by e-mail. Accordingly, adjuncts currently receive e-mail copies of the AFAC meeting minutes once a month and a newsletter every other month that highlights upcoming events, training, and recognition of outstanding contributions by specific adjuncts. AFAC also has a site on the Kirkwood Information Network for adjuncts to access information. The content is controlled by AFAC through the AFAC communications coordinator. Professional development events and activities are advertised through Kirkwood's TEMPO daily Internet posting.

Opportunities for engagement with full-time faculty are also available to adjuncts in order to foster the community. As standard practice, adjunct instructors are now invited to almost all Kirkwood and faculty departmental meetings and included on all college communications. The Kirkwood administration invites adjuncts to participate in annual, college-wide Collaborative Learning Days to work with full-time faculty in skill development and focused discussions. Participation in the noncontract days learning opportunities is encouraged through monetary stipends of $100 per day. Through KCELT, adjuncts are also able to propose and facilitate their own professional development sessions for other adjuncts or tenured faculty, which demonstrates the college's recognition of their capability as educators.

Finally, Kirkwood makes an effort to include adjuncts in the campus community by recognizing their dedicated service to the college. In April of every year, Kirkwood administration and AFAC host a Spring Garden Party at which the president of the college and the vice president of academic affairs are present to share their thoughts and hand out certificates and gift cards to recognize adjuncts for every five years of service. The event is catered with a variety of refreshments.

In Summary

On the basis of the November 2014 AFAC annual survey, the Kirkwood adjunct community continues to have a very positive attitude toward Kirkwood and how adjuncts are supported. Adjuncts are largely satisfied with their treatment at Kirkwood because the college recognizes the value of its adjunct community and thus strives to provide a comprehensive system of support structures to improve adjuncts' integration into the community and enhance their quality of life. Developing quality adjunct faculty is an ongoing and evolving process to which Kirkwood is committed. The result of Kirkwood's commitment to its adjuncts is improvement in the integration and development of its faculty and thus improvement in learning for all Kirkwood students.

11

Cultivating Scholarly Teaching Through Professional Development

Ann Coburn-Collins, Anne M. Acker, Lester L. Altevogt, and Lisa S. Tsay

How do we grow scholarly teachers, especially adjunct faculty, given that faculty development opportunities and the principle financial resources, such as the Scholarship of Teaching and Learning (SoTL) grants, are typically not available for part-time faculty? Despite such obstacles, adjunct faculty development is important because research focusing on adjunct faculty and their teaching practices have demonstrated a number of undesirable outcomes. For instance, one study found that students who had increased contact to part-time faculty in their first semester were more likely to have declining GPAs and lower credit-hour completion in their second semester (Harrington & Schibik, 2004), and Ehrenberg and Zhang (2004) found that student graduation rates decline when exposure to adjunct faculty increases. Eagan and Jaeger (2009) also found that community college students who had mostly part-time faculty were less likely to transfer to four-year institutions. Some of these factors can be explained by the relative lack of professional development opportunities and classroom teaching assessments done primarily by students (Kezar & Maxey, 2013). A further explanation for these undesirable outcomes may be the dismal working conditions and social environments in which many adjunct faculty are expected to teach. It is, therefore, inherently important that colleges and universities bring into focus the idea of providing classroom support and cultivating improved teaching practices for their adjunct faculty through professional development opportunities.

Saginaw Valley State University (SVSU) prides itself on being a premier teaching institution. Recognizing the issues related to the support of adjunct faculty in the classroom, SVSU, in its 2005 Strategic Plan, took action by creating the Office of Adjunct Faculty Support Programs. The mission of this program is to provide faculty development and classroom support for the university's adjunct faculty population and for those departments who employ them. Since its inception, this program has employed best practices to ensure that the university's adjunct faculty receive quality support. Specifically, this program has used Lyons and Burnstad's (2007) best practices to design programs intended to foster the teaching practices for our adjunct faculty and to cultivate scholarly teaching through the use of evidenced-based methods. These best practices include (a) a thorough orientation to the institution, (b) adequate training in fundamental teaching and classroom management skills, (c) ongoing professional development opportunities, and (d) recognition for adjunct faculty quality work (Lyons & Burnstad, 2007).

A Thorough Orientation to the Institution

Our program offers a thorough orientation to SVSU each August, three weeks before the start of classes, and then again before the start of the winter term. This fall orientation is extensive, offering numerous opportunities for those who participate. The orientation begins early in the day with a combined meeting between the new full- and part-time faculty and representatives from the university's support services, who explain their role in supporting students. Later, the faculty are offered an opportunity to be trained on the university's learning management system (LMS). Next the faculty meet with their dean and department chairs to discuss assessment and accreditation issues. Then, in the early evening, faculty are invited to dine with their deans and chairs. After dinner, the adjunct faculty attend three 45-minute breakout sessions. New adjunct faculty are required to attend a session with the program's director to learn about the university's policies and procedures related to their employment. Topics for the other professional development breakout sessions include classroom management, first day of class, teaching international students, and universal design, to name a few.

To orient new faculty hired to teach in the winter term, the program offers a small meet and greet in its office, where policies and procedures are discussed and any questions are answered. Additional components of both of these orientations involves the dissemination of the Adjunct Faculty Handbook, information about upcoming workshops opportunities, a list of questions for adjuncts to ask their department chairs, and any other information that is pertinent to their teaching success. The orientations are not required, yet a considerable number of adjunct faculty attend. The fall orientation usually attracts about 40% (about 190 people) of the university's adjunct faculty, many of whom attend all of the events offered on orientation day. For the 2014 winter orientation last year, about 50% of the new faculty were in attendance.

Adequate Training in Fundamental Teaching and Classroom Management Skills

Other professional development opportunities that this program provides fulfill the best practices related to training in fundamental teaching and classroom management skills. The program's intent is to educate the adjunct faculty in evidenced-based teaching practices as a means of improving teaching and learning in the classroom. Monthly workshops and brown-bag lunches are offered using such thematic topics as use of high-impact practices (Kuh, 2009) and classroom engagement techniques. These workshops average an attendance of about 15 adjunct faculty. In addition, course design workshops are offered each semester on three Saturday mornings over the course of three months. The course design workshops help faculty members create learning outcomes for their classes, develop active learning lessons, and design their course syllabi. The course design workshops usually attract about six faculty members each semester. Each year, a Summer Technology Institute, attended by about 20 faculty members, is offered, allowing the instructors time to learn about or hone their skills with the university's LMS and become familiar with pedagogically sound uses of technology for the purposes of teaching and learning. Because the program is a single point of service for the university's adjunct faculty, it is possible to also get on-demand course consultations with a faculty developer. All of these professional development opportunities are intended to provide the university's adjunct faculty with the tools to affect student success. One faculty member who consistently attends the monthly workshops offered the following reflection:

> For me, the workshops have provided two great benefits. The first is that I always seem to find encouragement from them. If I am struggling a bit during the semester, they offer a fresh perspective on teaching and always give me boost. The second benefit is the reaction I get from my students after I try out a new technique in my classroom that I learned from a workshop. I have always been an active, hands-on teacher, but I have learned and utilized so many new techniques learned in the monthly workshops that I see the improvement in students' understanding.

Ongoing Professional Development Opportunities

In addition to these monthly workshops and other professional development opportunities, there are three fairly intensive professional development opportunities available through the program. Each professional development opportunity is intended to help the adjunct faculty develop scholarly practices and improve student success. The first is a peer-mentoring program called LEAD, in which a full-time faculty member is asked to mentor a part-time faculty member during the fall and winter semesters. These pairs meet monthly to discuss teaching philosophies, course design, assessment, and so on. They attend each other's classes, and in the end, the adjunct faculty member creates an online portfolio that contains his or her teaching philosophy and teaching history. During this two-semester program, the participants are also asked to attend at least three workshops each semester. The relationships that are built as a result of this mentoring program are important and long lasting. Often mentor pairs are seen having coffee together, long after their completion of this program. As of 2017, 24 adjunct faculty have completed the LEAD program.

The second professional development opportunity is the Adjunct Faculty Funding Program, where faculty who plan to attend or present at a conference, seminar, auxiliary training, and so on can complete an Individual Development Plan (IDP). The IDP asks them to assess their perceived strengths and weaknesses in their teaching practices. They are then asked how their attendance at this professional meeting or training might affect their teaching. Upon returning from the event, they submit a report that summarizes what they learned at the meeting and how they will put what they learned at the event into practice. Each year, on average, eight adjunct faculty take advantage of this funding opportunity.

The third professional development opportunity is an Adjunct Faculty Learning Community (AFLC), established in the fall semester of 2013. This AFLC focuses on the practice of teaching first-year students. Because adjunct faculty teach many first-year courses, our program decided that developing an AFLC would help enhance and improve their teaching. So far, three faculty participants have joined the community. These faculty are from mathematical sciences, philosophy, and psychology. After completing an IDP asking them to reflect on their perceived pedagogical strengths and weaknesses, the participants began the program by attending the Lilly Conference in Traverse City, Michigan, to learn about the SoTL. The theme for the Lilly Conferences surrounds "Evidence-Based Teaching and Learning," which was a perfect venue to teach new faculty about SoTL. Following the Lilly Conference, the AFLC members decided on what classroom research they would like to pursue in order to improve their teaching and student outcomes. SVSU's Institutional Review Board (IRB) approval for the entire community was acquired, and the research began. After the completion of their first year of research, the community members returned to the Lilly Conference in 2014 to present the results of their scholarship.

As of this writing, the community members continue to meet monthly, and their research is ongoing. For instance, one faculty member began her research by measuring the effect that active learning has on improved learning outcomes (Coburn-Collins, Acker, Altevogt, & Tsay, 2014). She found that her experimental group that received active learning practices achieved better grades than her students in the control group did, who did no active learning. Her current research question is to quantitatively measure the effect that active learning combined with homework has on better grades. The success of the AFLC is due in large part to the dedication of the faculty members and the support they give to one another. As one faculty member put it,

> The AFLC supports the educator's ideal that it isn't enough to have a firm understanding of the content and the objectives for a course in this university; one has to engage the learner so that the opportunity to learn the content abounds in one's course. The goal of the educator is to have results in one's teaching. Having the Community supported by the IRB keeps the goal of improving the learners' worldview focused for the educator.

Our program created two new offerings for the fall 2015 semester. Because our orientation reaches only 40% of the adjunct faculty, we are launching an online orientation for those who cannot or do not attend the on-campus event. In addition, we will be initiating an Adjunct Faculty Seminar for those adjunct faculty who have taught at the university for three or fewer semesters. The seminar will meet every other week for 10 weeks for an hour and a half. The curriculum for the seminar includes learning about evidence-based teaching practices, appropriate methods for classroom management and assessment, the creation of collegial relationships among the faculty, the characteristics of SVSU's student body, and the university's culture.

Recognition for Adjunct Faculty Quality Work

The final best practice is recognition for adjunct faculty quality work that has been identified as "appropriate and adequate" (Lyons & Burnstad, 2007). Essentially, the university recognizes our adjunct faculty through compensation. Workshop participants are compensated $25 per workshop for up to four workshops each semester. They are also compensated $50 for their attendance at the orientations and for their participation in the course design workshops and Summer Technology Institutes. Those who participate in LEAD are compensated each semester at a rate of $250, and once the mentoring is complete, they receive a $50 bump in their per-credit-hour pay. The AFLC has had its fees and travel expenses to the Lilly Conference, in both

2013 and 2014, paid for by our program, which exceeded $1,000 for each participant. Finally, at the end of each academic year, our program organizes an award's banquet. The banquet includes dinner, drinks, and a band. Years of service plaques are awarded to those teaching 5, 10, 15, and more years at the university, and the faculty member who earns the adjunct faculty member of the year award is recognized.

It is difficult to quantitatively assess the success of such programs. SVSU's Office of Institutional Research (OIR), for instance, looked into the "first time in college" (FTIC) retention rate for both full- and part-time faculty and found a 1% difference between the two groups. In addition, the OIR was asked to compare the retention rates and grades of the LEAD participants two semesters prior to LEAD and the two semesters following LEAD. The OIR looked at only a few of the participants' classes and found that the post-LEAD semester retention rates and students' grades improved over the pre-LEAD semester rates and grades. This brief study does not necessarily reflect on the entire group of LEAD graduates. However, qualitative data suggest the members of the adjunct faculty who participate in our programs state how their classes have improved and that they have developed collegial relationships with one another, whose chief topic of conversation is teaching and learning. Often, in our office, we overhear faculty saying, "How was class today?" indicating that teaching has become center stage in the life of the adjunct faculty at SVSU. To us, this reflects that the programs based on Lyons and Burnstad's (2007) best practices have helped to cultivate and grow the teaching practices of our adjunct faculty.

References

Coburn-Collins, A., Acker, A., Altevogt, L., & Tsay, L. (2014, October). *An Adjunct Faculty Learning Community to increase intentional learning.* Paper presented at the Lilly Conference, Traverse City, MI.

Eagan, M. K., & Jaegar, A. J. (2009). Effects of exposure to part-time faculty on community college transfer. *Research in Higher Education, 50*(2), 168–188. doi:10.1007/s11162-008-9113-8

Ehrenberg, R., & Zhang, L. (2004). *Do tenured and tenure-track faculty matter?* (Working Paper No. 10695). Cambridge, MA: National Bureau of Economic Research. doi:10.3386/w10695

Harrington, C., & Schibik, T. (2004). Caveat emptor: Is there a relationship between part-time faculty utilization and student learning retention? *Association for Institutional Research, 91*, 1–10. Retrieved from http://admin.airweb.org/EducationAndEvents/Publications/ProfessionalFiles/Documents/91.pdf

Kezar, A., & Maxey, D. (2013). *Dispelling the myths: Locating the resources to support non-tenure-track faculty* (Report). The Delphi Project on the Changing Faculty and Student Success. Retrieved from http://www.uscrossier.org/pullias/wp-content/uploads/2013/10/DelphiProject-Dispelling_the_Myths.pdf

Kuh, G. (2009). *High-impact educational practices, what they are, who has access to them, and why they matter.* Washington, DC: Association of American Colleges & Universities.

Lyons, R. E., & Burnstad, H. (2007). *Best practices for supporting adjunct faculty.* Paper presented at the Chair Academy's Annual Conference, Jacksonville, FL.

12

The Transformative Effects of an Adjunct Faculty Academy

One Approach to Teaching Adjuncts Pedagogy, Instructional Design, and Best Practices

Summer Cherland, Heather Crook, Lindsey Dippold, J.W. Gaberdiel, and Jenalee Remy

In September 2014, six adjunct faculty instructors at GateWay Community College received unexpected phone calls, all inviting them to participate in the inaugural "Excellence in Teaching" Adjunct Faculty Academy (AFA). The following is a summary of the academy written collaboratively by four of the participants and one organizer. We will begin with the foundations of the AFA, describing its origins, its funding sources, and how participants were nominated by campus leaders to participate. Each of the four symposia will be described from the perspective of one of the participants. Each faculty member will outline the learning objectives and lessons taught in the session, as well as explain how he or she put those lessons to use immediately in the classroom. We will conclude with our hopes for the future of this academy and suggestions for other campuses and faculty developers considering this type of support structure for adjunct faculty. Although we are proud of our experiences and feel strongly that the AFA was a significant source of support and professional development, we will also include some recommendations for improvement.

Although the AFA focused primarily on pedagogical skills, the most noteworthy result was that each participant felt increased empowerment and took on greater leadership within the community after attending. We spent a combined 25 hours together, discussing best practices, observing each other's classes, and then collaborating on this chapter; throughout this process, each of us became more confident in our individual roles as campus leaders. The assumption might be that adjunct faculty are an unseen, unacknowledged majority on a community college campus, and while the AFA provided a community of support for adjunct faculty, it also ingrained in us the confidence to become that community of support for our peers. We will discuss this transformation by providing individual perspectives regarding leadership, community, and support following our participation in the academy.

The "Excellence in Teaching" AFA was a semester-long partnership among GateWay's Center for Teaching and Learning (CTL), the Maricopa County Community College District (MCCCD), and the Adjunct Faculty Association. GateWay is located in Phoenix, Arizona, and is one of 10 Maricopa community colleges. The following statement captures GateWay's identity:

> Since 1968, GateWay Community College has built a legacy of innovation, pioneering vision, and responsiveness to the needs of our community— being the first technical college in Arizona; first to use community advisory committees; first to tailor courses to the needs of business and industry; first to offer classes at off-campus locations; even the first to install a computer. From a humble beginning in the former Korrick's Department Store downtown, Maricopa Technical College has flourished over the past 40 years into today's GateWay Community College. (Gateway Community College, n.d.)

We can add another first to the list: GateWay is the first campus in the Maricopa District to offer the AFA. Having heard great feedback from participants regarding the networking opportunities, technological training, and increased confidence in the classroom that resulted from the academy, three additional Maricopa campuses have initiated collaboration, which will bring the training program to a regional and statewide audience, led by GateWay's CTL staff.

We hope our description of the academy will demonstrate the genuine respect we have for the program and express our suggestions and considerations for future like-minded endeavors for faculty, campus leaders, and faculty developers.

Description of the "Excellence in Teaching" Adjunct Faculty Academy

Over the past several years, academic reliance on adjunct faculty has continued to increase, especially at the community college level. Although more courses are taught by adjunct faculty than by residential faculty within the MCCCD, professional development opportunities designed for adjunct faculty vary by campus and often do not cover essential teaching skills such as lesson planning, active learning strategies, and the design of course assessments (many offerings do, however, address basic learning management system [LMS] online technology, classroom management, and basic procedural requirements).

A recent MCCCD initiative calls for more attention to be given to training and developing adjunct faculty, especially in the developmental education areas that have the lowest retention rates. With the permission and support from the campus president at GateWay, the director of the CTL and the campus AFA representative collaborated to design a pilot program that would address these needs. Although training along these objectives had been designed in 2008 at the district level, its momentum subsequently faded. For the current program, a similar curriculum was used, but many new elements were addressed, including delivery method, sample size, and group culture. For GateWay's academy, participants met one Saturday morning per month during the fall semester, for a total of five meetings, lasting about five hours each session. Online interaction and peer observations took place in between, encouraging reflection and additional learning and fostering participant collaboration. The pilot program included adjunct faculty who were nominated by department chairs and had each taught in the district for fewer than three years. In total, only six participants were included, ensuring one-on-one attention and in-depth collaboration. These participants represented an array of disciplines across the campus, including English, counseling, communications, mathematics, history, and psychology. Each participant was contacted with the opportunity to participate at the beginning of the semester and informed of the time required. Upon beginning the program, the program administrators provided a course syllabus and detailed the structure, format, and objectives for the participants.

The goals of the program included the following:

1. Provide in-depth coverage of key areas of pedagogy, curriculum design, and instructional best practices that are not included in required training in order to improve the effectiveness of adjunct faculty, especially in developmental areas or areas with lower retention rates
2. Connect participants with local campus resources, build community, and better inform them about campus culture, including the opportunities and challenges of the specific campus
3. Aid in the promotion of adjunct faculty who demonstrate additional commitment to the practice and institution by providing opportunities to network and exposure to future campus searches for residential faculty

Session 1: Setting the Stage, From the Perspective of Summer Cherland

The purpose of the first session was to lay the groundwork for a successful academy. It began with an intriguing presentation by college administrators regarding our campus culture. The demographics, retention statistics, and matriculation predictions of our student population were identified and described to this group of adjunct instructors. Although much of this information is provided on the campus website and within internal publications, adjunct faculty generally do not have consistent opportunities to access this information.

We continued with a teaching-and-learning-style assessment, which was significant for those faculty members who had never learned about their own teaching styles. From there, we applied our learning and teaching styles to the lesson planning process. Participants were asked in advance to bring their syllabi and a sample lesson to the session. Then participants identified areas within their lessons that applied to their preferred teaching style. Multiple sample lesson plans from colleagues were provided, with tools and resources for improving the way we plan our lessons. For example, the director of the CTL shared some of his best practices in lesson planning, and CTL instructional designers provided examples of their own successful lessons. Additional professional lesson plans were shared, and participants were asked to redesign a recent class of their own to better serve the needs of their students.

Upon conclusion of this session, participants were asked to reflect on and apply what they learned in this session. Because own lesson planning strategies were already well established, I used this opportunity to critique my lessons and consider if my teaching styles appealed to the multimodal styles of my students. While I might be an auditory learner, many of my students might need varied techniques and activities to learn productively. Because of the work completed in the first session, I spent the next two semesters diligently designing my lessons with inclusion in mind.

Session 2: Connecting and Engaging, From the Perspective of J. W. Gaberdiel

The intent of the second session was to demonstrate the link between student engagement and learning retention. By reaching out to adjunct faculty, who represent a significant majority of instructors, organizers believed that student retention and success could be increased. The workshop began with a presentation regarding the link between student engagement and learning retention, along with real-life examples of how low engagement, passive learning, and low motivation can interfere with the learning process. Next, the session introduced active learning techniques and questioning strategies. Participants practiced both, including storytelling, reflection, and jigsaw learning strategies. Finally, a guest speaker who specialized in classroom management and civility spoke to the importance of active learning techniques to meet course competencies and encourage student retention and respect.

This lesson provided many hands-on opportunities that could be incorporated immediately in the classroom. Some of the simplest suggestions showed instant results, such as switching statements into questions to allow students the opportunity to reflect. Stretching my lectures, instead of rushing them, and pausing for progress were also strategies suggested in the session. Most significant, one of the program directors scheduled a time to visit my classroom to provide me with direct feedback regarding how I used active learning in my classroom.

Session 3: How We Know They Are Learning, From the Perspective of Jenalee Remy

In the third section of the AFA, we focused on the role of assessment in the classroom. This lesson specifically addressed the importance of student assessment and how we, as faculty, can determine the retention level of individuals in our classrooms. During this session, participants engaged in an activity that interactively engaged the trainees in distinguishing between *formative* and *summative* assessment techniques. Formative, referring to assessment during the course that guides instructors in making modifications in their teaching, can include focus groups and in-class questions that ask for feedback. Summative, indicating evaluation of student learning at the end of a section of the course, can be done through an exam or project (Chappuis, 2009). The speaker then focused on *alignment*, or how closely the lesson mirrors the course objectives. This was demonstrated through the usage of the modules tool located on the Canvas website. Following this exercise, participants created lesson plans in congruence with the combined alignment of relevancy to each adjunct's course. Last, the speaker demonstrated use of a rubric and guided participants through the process and theory of rubric-based evaluation.

I chose to implement this lesson most notably by creating and implementing the use of rubrics for my class's upcoming project. I enlisted the CTL's help in coming up with appropriate wording that would clearly describe the criteria to be evaluated and effectively create objective and accurate measurements of the various elements. The result was an elaborate rubric that objectively captured the items needed and reflected the alignment of the objectives and course intent. Through this guidance, I was able to vary the levels of completeness the students may have used in their writing and presenting and grade accordingly. This lesson was immediately useful to my classroom and course development. As a result of this exercise, my grading was much easier and more time efficient, and I felt more confident in the congruency of my grading among students.

Session 4: Putting It All Together, From the Perspective of Heather Crook

For the fourth session, we discussed what had changed for us over the course of the semester, went over a series of teaching tips, had a final session on using our LMS, and looked at some ideas for day one icebreaker activities in the classroom. "Putting It All Together" provided an overview of the entire semester's lessons. We began with an intensive training session, intended to make us experts in navigating the LMS, Canvas. From there, we surveyed the past 16 weeks of data and designed our course syllabus, paying attention to setting ground rules and behavioral expectations in our learning communities. The first day of the semester was also presented as an important opportunity to create the learning environment and encourage student interaction. We learned that introductions and syllabus review can be interactive and intentional. We discussed Michael Brady's (2008) "Teaching Tips" as a clincher to our time together.

Brady's "Teaching Tips" struck a chord with me. Personally, I am not afraid to be human with my students, but I realize that is a comfort zone many professors do not wish to leave. As for enjoying our students, well, I don't think any of us would have been there if we weren't truly passionate about what we do already. For most of us, I think, the semester had certainly brought in a wind of change and a breath of fresh air to our curriculum. I had several ideas with which to begin the following semester and was itching to implement them.

Future Directions

The success of the pilot program of the Adjunct Faculty Academy was clear to both participants and facilitators. The academy will be hosted by GateWay again this coming fall, with an increase in participants, from 6 to 10. The intention is to reach a larger number of adjunct faculty members with this essential training, while still cultivating an intimate community. This builds strong relationships, provides individualized attention and feedback, and offers meaningful teaching observations. In addition to continuing to offer and grow the academy on GateWay's campus, the facilitators are collaborating with the district office to create a district-wide version of the academy, with general pedagogical sessions as a larger group and supplemental breakout sessions offered at each participating campus. This approach will streamline resources for main sessions while allowing academy participants the opportunity to become better acquainted with their specific campus resources and the campus culture, as it varies by campus.

References

Brady, E. M. (2008). Teaching tips: Teaching strategies for graduate students and teaching assistants. [Lecture]. Florida State University.

Chappuis, J. (2009). *Seven strategies of assessment for learning*. Boston, MA: Pearson.

GateWay Community College. (n.d.). About. Retrieved from http://www.gatewaycc.edu/about

13

Best Practices and Innovative Faculty Development for Adjunct Faculty

Ruth Fagan

In 2002 at our Research I university's top-ranked School of Social Work, it became evident that the use of adjunct faculty had become an essential component in the delivery of the school's academic program. This mirrored a national trend: "Between 1976–2005 contingent [adjunct] faculty increased by more than 200% in higher education whereas over the same period full-time tenured and tenure-track faculty grew by only 17%" (American Association of University Professors, 2008, p. 17). In fact, by 2002, 40% of the social work classes in both our undergraduate and graduate social work programs were being taught by adjunct faculty, many of whom also held clinical or social policy positions in the community and/or in the state (Fagan-Wilen, Springer, Ambrosino, & White, 2006).

Noting this trend in our department and being an adjunct faculty member myself, I began advocating for a way to better support our adjuncts in improved teaching, which was also the topic of my doctoral research (Fagan-Wilen, 1995). Being aware that the majority of our adjunct instructors came and went primarily in the evening, with little or no real connection to the broader university or departmental community, I went to the dean to propose the creation of an *adjunct faculty liaison* position—to provide leadership and structure aimed at the recruitment, training, and support of these essential faculty.

In the 13 years since the inception of this adjunct support program, the adjunct liaison position and ancillary adjunct supports have been modified, grown in breadth and delivery, and strengthened. We have gone from 32 adjunct faculty in 2002 to 50 in 2015, with many serving on academic and curricula committees within the department, collaborating with tenure and tenure-track faculty teaching the same course or similar courses, and frequently using the wealth of teaching resources offered by the university at large.

There are several overarching themes related to this growth: (a) recruitment and training; (b) support in the classroom with both curricula and student performance; and (c) most important, an increased *appreciation and awareness* by the tenure and tenure-track faculty of the value and strength that adjuncts bring to the quality of the academics taught. I will discuss each of these themes, highlighting best practices and innovative faculty development in each.

Recruitment and Training

The logistical challenges of ensuring quality class teaching coverage to over 700 social work undergraduate and graduate social work students, per semester, within a Research I university can be daunting. This challenge normally falls squarely on the shoulders of the associate dean and is necessarily complicated when nationally recognized tenure and tenure-track faculty are awarded major research and funding grants, requiring reduced teaching loads—sometimes with notice given just a few weeks prior to the semester start. To be prepared to cover all classes requires not only a large number of qualified adjunct faculty but also, for professional education, a pool of adjuncts with high levels of expertise in specific clinical practice or policy areas.

As social work professional education requires both academic preparation and semester-long student field placements in social service, mental health, and policy-based organizations, recruiting talented field instructors from these agencies and programs as possible prospective adjunct faculty can provide an added benefit. In fact, the associate dean and adjunct liaison are in diligent "recruiting" mode a good deal of the time. The challenge here is that not all of our pool of qualified adjuncts will be called on to teach every semester, so the liaison must convey clear communication and support to those *not* teaching in any given semester, a role as important in the recruitment process as clear and timely communication and support to those who will be teaching.

Training was by far the most important cornerstone of the adjunct support program begun in 2002—and it remains so. Although adjunct instructors in all domains are hired because of their highly regarded practice or policy expertise in the subject area, they often have had little or no teaching experience. Knowing that they will receive ongoing, specific support in developing and delivering good classroom teaching skills is often what allows new adjunct instructors to step up and embrace this new, somewhat daunting role. This support includes (a) a comprehensive orientation prior to the semester, either one-on-one or in a small group, to university and departmental infrastructure and general policies; (b) help with syllabus development including texts, assignments, exam development, grading rubrics, and use of classroom technology; (c) collaboration with other faculty who have taught or are teaching a section of the same class; (d) yearly teaching skills trainings co-led with the University Center for Teaching and Learning; (e) monthly brown-bag informal lunches for adjuncts to come and share with each other *any* teaching issues they may be having that semester; and (f) IT evening training once a semester conducted by an assigned university IT person focused on ever-changing new classroom information technologies, such as Blackboard and Canvas. An unanticipated but very welcome by-product of this range of trainings is the sense of community that has developed among the adjuncts—"We're all in this together." They share meals, learn, and problem solve classroom strategies together.

Support

It became clear that to retain the commitment and enthusiasm of high-performing adjunct faculty, as demonstrated by their consistently high course instructor student evaluations, several supports needed to be offered. First, instructors were given the opportunity to teach two courses per semester if they so chose—this had not been done before. This increased recognition for their teaching expertise and provided added income and some employee benefits. Second, we were able to assign a part-time graduate teaching assistant (TA) specifically for adjuncts to help with classroom preparations, resources, library searches, and assistance with grading in the undergraduate classes. The TA is also available online to receive requests so that when the adjunct arrives on campus, often shortly prior to class, their requested work is ready and waiting—an incredible benefit. Third, the liaison is available to meet on or off campus at the convenience of the adjunct, throughout the semester, to discuss classroom issues related to course assignments and/or concerns about students. These meetings may be in person or by phone, and adjuncts have commented frequently on the availability of this support as motivation to continue teaching even after a difficult or challenging semester. Some specific adjunct comments support this availability:

> Any department needs leadership. UT assures that happens by hiring a faculty/staff liaison just for the adjunct community. When I came into the school, it was this person that helped integrate me into the processes and practices at UTSSW. This leadership position affords us the oppor-

tunity to discuss difficult issues in the classroom, challenging student issues, and acts as a broker for providing input and suggestions to the full [social work] department. (S. Miller, adjunct faculty, quotation from written classroom observation, University of Texas at Austin School of Social Work, April 2015)

The creation of the adjunct faculty liaison position has been instrumental. . . . I recall a time when this position did not exist, and it often resulted in adjunct faculty feeling anxious, isolated, and ineffective. It's difficult to teach under these circumstances. I see the support of adjunct faculty as an academic imperative, and after ten years of working closely with the adjunct liaison, remain convinced that this is a critical position for any program that takes seriously its commitment to educate students. (D. Springer, associate dean from 2002–2012, quotation regarding the impact of the School of Social Work Adjunct Faculty Support Program, April 2015)

Another recent addition to our support program is the liaison's availability to *observe* the adjunct in the classroom—this is done at the adjunct's request, and specific, confidential feedback is provided to improve teaching. Here are responses received from adjuncts after the observation:

In over 30 years of teaching at different universities/colleges, this is the first time a faculty/peer actually observed one of my classes. I plan to integrate the adjunct faculty liaison's comments into my class flow next semester. . . . Thank you so much for taking the time and effort to enhance my teaching skills. I think this is a great example of adding value to adjunct faculty instructors! (G. Jensen, adjunct faculty, quotation from written classroom observation, University of Texas at Austin School of Social Work, April 2014)

This was a very useful experience for me! It helps in one's teaching to be reminded of what it looks like from the outside, to get feedback about what works well and about where continued growth and learning can happen. . . . The comments the adjunct liaison made before and after class gave me much to think about. This experience was even a bit reenergizing for my teaching! (anonymous adjunct faculty instructor, quotation from written classroom observation, University of Texas at Austin School of Social Work, April 2014)

Because the observation feedback is private and only for the adjunct, the process has not been seen as threatening or intrusive, and in fact, tenure-track faculty have begun requesting classroom teaching observations as well.

Appreciation and Awareness

Adjunct faculty have often been considered "invisible"—they go and come when other faculty are not on campus and may not be known even when they appear at faculty functions. This lack of appreciation and awareness has been remedied in our school in a number of ways.

First, we instituted a "Lecturer Teaching Excellence Award," which recognizes one outstanding adjunct faculty per year. The award is announced and celebrated at the same end-of-the year event at which the coveted tenure and tenure-track teaching award is presented. Concomitant with this recognition, a tiered salary scale was implemented providing salary raises for senior outstanding adjunct faculty. Second, making the "invisible" visible, we include by invitation *all* adjunct faculty to all major departmental academic and celebratory events. This includes national speaker presentations; faculty research colloquia; and, most important, holiday and graduation events where faculty, students, and staff come together in a common community. Adjunct faculty had in the past not been included at these events—this change has brought about a marked improvement in *overall* faculty morale. This systemic change toward inclusion has been supported by faculty, tenured and adjunct alike. In fact, a collaboration between a distinguished tenured professor and a clinician adjunct faculty resulted in coauthorship of a prominent clinical casebook text now widely used in graduate social work and mental health programs throughout the country (Pomeroy & Garcia, 2010).

Impact of Adjunct Faculty Support

In 2010, our school conducted an exit study asking graduating master of social work (MSW) students to rate the quality of classroom instruction received from both tenure and tenure-track instructors and adjunct instructors. The study found no statistically significant differences between the overall ratings of the two faculty (D. Springer, associate dean from 2002–2010, exit survey of MSW students, University of Texas at Austin School of Social Work, 2010). On a different questionnaire using open-ended questions focused on teaching effectiveness, social work graduate students stated they highly valued adjunct instructors who "can bring real-world cases and experiences into classroom learning" (Fagan-Wilen et al., 2006, p. 47). In addition to strong student support for adjunct instruction, it has become clear that *retention* of adjunct faculty has improved: Out of 50 adjunct instructors presently available to teach, 42 (84%) have taught for 3 to 15 years in our program, providing vital ongoing stability to the academic program and consistency of quality instruction. In the past as many as 8 to 10 instructors in the fall were first-time adjuncts. This number has decreased to 2 to 3 first-time instructors, with the majority of classes covered by experienced adjuncts and tenure and tenure-track faculty.

The Future

Adjunct faculty salaries, nationwide, remain a difficult, challenging problem (Barnshaw & Dunietz, 2015). Although we have a two-tiered promotion system for experienced adjunct faculty, the starting per-class adjunct salary still remains too low. In addition, because of fluctuations in class enrollment, last-minute tenure-track faculty teaching buyouts, and the adjuncts' own full-time professional commitments, adjunct faculty do not always get timely notice or cannot plan for future teaching contracts. We remain committed to rectifying these issues; what we have learned from students, from tenure and tenure-track faculty, and from deans within our campus and nationally is that adjunct faculty in many ways represent the direction of higher education teaching in the future and must be so acknowledged.

> I know that I have personally learned as much from our school's adjunct faculty, if not more, than they have learned from me. (D. Springer, associate dean from 2002–2010, quotation from exit survey of MSW students, University of Texas at Austin School of Social Work, 2010)

References

American Association of University Professors. (2008). The annual report on the economic status of the profession, 2007–2008. *Academe, 94*(2), 8–86. Retrieved from http://www.jstor.org/stable/40253178

Barnshaw, J., & Dunietz, S. (2015). Busting the myth: The annual report on the economic status of the profession, 2014–2015. *Academe, 101*(2), 4–18. Retrieved from http://www.aaup.org/sites/default/files/files/2015salarysurvey/zreport.pdf

Fagan-Wilen, R. (1995). *Evaluating effective teaching in graduate schools of social work: Criteria used by graduate students and faculty* (Unpublished doctoral dissertation). University of Texas School of Social Work, Austin, TX.

Fagan-Wilen, R., Springer, D., Ambrosino, B., & White, B. (2006). The support of adjunct faculty: An academic imperative. *Social Work Education, 25*, 30–51.

Pomeroy, E., & Garcia, R. (2010). *The grief assessment and intervention workbook.* Belmont CA: Brooks/Cole Cengage Learning.

Conclusion

Toward Making the Invisible Visible, Heard, and Valued

Roy Fuller

For the title of their 1993 groundbreaking study of adjunct faculty, Judith M. Gappa and David W. Leslie chose *The Invisible Faculty* to draw attention to the many adjunct faculty whose presence was little known outside the institutions they served. These highly educated individuals labored in conditions that were often invisible—even to those inside the academy. Fast-forward 20 years, and we have sought to highlight the stories of adjunct faculty who—although more visible than perhaps ever before—are nonetheless typically found on the sidelines of a heated debate regarding their role and the value of their contributions. As our contributors and survey respondents have demonstrated, adjunct faculty are often treated as marginal employees, with little or no job security and poor working conditions. This reality is disturbing, because adjunct faculty now compose the largest segment of the teaching academic workforce and are charged with the lion's share of introductory and general education courses at many institutions (Coalition on the Academic Workforce, 2012; Kezar, 2012).

The challenges facing higher education today are complex and extend beyond issues related to adjunct faculty. Indeed, the central enterprise of how we teach so that our students can learn and be successful upon graduation—the heart of American higher education—is under attack. Public sector dollars flowing toward higher education have been declining for decades, and bringing in research dollars is more important for faculty seeking tenure and promotion. This state of affairs has pushed the pursuit of teaching excellence to the periphery at many institutions. What then of those in the academic workforce whose work is devoted *exclusively* to teaching, namely, adjunct faculty? How might these individuals be empowered rather than marginalized?

Along with increases in the use of adjunct and contingent faculty, we find it concerning that the 2015–2016 American Association of University Professors (AAUP) report, *Higher Education at a Crossroads: The Annual Report on the Economic Status of the Profession, 2015–16,* made this claim regarding adjunct faculty:

While many faculty members serving in part-time positions are well qualified and *make extraordinary efforts to overcome their circumstances*, [emphasis
added] researchers have found that having a part-time instructor decreases
the likelihood that a student will take subsequent classes in a subject and
that instruction by part-time faculty is negatively associated with retention
and graduation. (AAUP, 2016, pp. 14–15)

This damning claim is made by professional organizations and advocacy groups who argue that adding full-time tenure positions will resolve a
number of issues. Given current hiring trends, we have no reason to believe
that fewer adjunct faculty will be hired in the foreseeable future. We argue
that one antidote to the AAUP's claim is for institutions to direct cost sav-
ings from hiring adjunct faculty to ensuring equitable treatment, access to
resources, and professional development opportunities. Student success is
increasingly becoming the standard measure for institutions of higher education. One proven way to increase student success rates is through high-
quality instruction, offered by faculty, whether full-time or part-time, who
have access to the resources they need to be the best teachers they can be.

In this book, we offer a snapshot of adjunct faculty at a single point
in time, looking at their demographics, working conditions, and efforts at
advocacy and organizing in seeking equitable treatment at the institutions
in which they work. Equally important are the voices of adjunct faculty who
have shared their stories of success and challenge in finding professional
development and community inside and outside the academy. Although
some accuse adjunct faculty members of passivity in regard to their working conditions and second-class status, our contributors' stories paint a different picture. These individuals have persevered, sought out professional
development opportunities, and become advocates for themselves and their
colleagues. For those who became faculty developers, they have brought a
powerful adjunct perspective to the way that faculty development is offered.

How do we make sense of what we have learned? We now offer a set of
themes with recommendations grouped into the following areas: identification, community building, equitable treatment, and professional development.

Identification

Higher education institutions must make it a priority to identify and communicate with their adjunct faculty members so that they can provide effective
support. Department chairs, course coordinators, deans, and faculty developers are often on the front lines of knowing which adjunct faculty have been
hired each term. Although they may not be in a position to offer professional

development opportunities at the department level, chairs are in a position to identify and connect adjunct faculty members with campus resources and information related to teaching, instructional design, and instructional technology. Securing access to the learning management system and training, e-mail, and other campus resources is essential for today's college teacher, yet many adjunct faculty report that they are locked out between terms. Chairs should also be responsible for conveying curricular information and course management expectations to *all* faculty. Unfortunately, this type of information is often not shared reliably and systematically.

At the same time that department chairs and others who supervise adjunct faculty need to maintain open lines of communication, adjunct faculty members must be empowered to find answers to their questions. Indeed, the temporary status of adjunct faculty may mean that they are not comfortable asking questions for fear of not being retained in favor of those who appear to do their work quietly without bothering anyone. Many institutions provide an adjunct faculty handbook containing relevant information about institutional systems, resources available, and development opportunities. The burden is on those seeking to support adjunct faculty to raise awareness of the existence of such resources and services.

As our survey demonstrated, many Centers for Teaching and Learning open some or all of their professional development programs to adjunct faculty, and although this is true, extra steps may be needed to ensure that adjunct faculty know they are welcome to take advantage of these programs. Well-targeted invitations and outreach efforts are the key. Department chairs and course coordinators are in a prime position to share opportunities and encourage adjunct faculty to participate in faculty development opportunities and acknowledge and reward those who do. Our faculty tell us that invitations and encouragement from chairs and colleagues are effective. In like manner, teaching centers and professional development offices should notify department chairs and others who employ adjunct faculty when adjunct faculty participate and complete professional development programs.

Communication is a two-way street. If colleges and universities desire a higher level of involvement and commitment from those who teach in adjunct capacities, these institutions in turn must demonstrate the same for their adjunct faculty. Faculty developers also need to listen to adjunct faculty to determine their specific needs and schedule offerings accordingly. This requires not only being able to identify and reach out to the adjunct community but also investing in gathering information about adjunct faculty through surveys, focus groups, and informal feedback. Adjunct faculty committees or other adjunct advocacy and organizations are ideal starting places. Knowing who adjunct faculty are is a start, but seeking to understand the specific needs of these various types of adjunct faculty offers campus leaders a road map for effecting positive change.

Community Building

The need for community is not limited to adjunct faculty, as many faculty find themselves teaching and working in isolation, each in their own "silo," even from other members in their own department. Such "siloing" has reduced both camaraderie and community and decreases the support systems for all faculty who need encouragement in making pedagogical changes in their teaching practice. Although some adjunct faculty are content to simply teach their classes with little or no contact with their institutions, interaction with colleagues is desirable for adjunct faculty whose courses are scheduled during evenings or weekends. Many adjunct faculty are excluded from department meetings. In addition, a growing number teach at multiple institutions. Considered together, these factors can lead adjuncts to professional fragmentation and disconnection from the communities in which they serve. Community building for faculty is an important component of professional development. Adjunct faculty, like all faculty, need encouragement and guidance as they hone their teaching by implementing new pedagogical strategies. A critical source of support for faculty when it comes to making changes in their teaching is fellow faculty members. The best faculty development opportunities seize on this fact and incorporate community building and sharing opportunities. When colleagues encourage adjunct faculty to try something new, learn from their successes and mistakes, and simply listen to their personal struggles in teaching, they make for better teaching.

Adjunct faculty have taken the initiative to create committees and organizations that can serve the dual purpose of making space for adjunct faculty to gather and function as advocacy organizations to the larger academic community. One way to reach across the boundaries that exist between adjunct faculty and full-time faculty is to use development programs that include both. Faculty learning communities, mentor programs, and peer classroom observations are all excellent ways to promote relationships among all segments of the faculty workforce and can provide all faculty with the sense of inclusion they often find lacking.

Equitable Treatment

Over the past few years, unions and other adjunct advocacy organizations have raised awareness about the poor working conditions under which many adjunct faculty labor. When issues of equity are raised, leaders may hear financial demands. Although equitable treatment for adjunct faculty would include addressing issues of insufficient compensation and a lack of standard benefits, equitable treatment should be viewed broadly. Beginning with the hiring process, adjunct faculty face a haphazard set of policies and practices surrounding their recruitment, selection, terms of employment, compensation, and evaluation, which is in contrast to other segments of the academic workforce who enjoy well-defined policies related to hiring, employment benefits, and evaluation. Although some of these issues can be dealt with through human resources, many can be addressed at the academic department level. Academic departments often follow the path of least resistance, stumbling upon adjunct faculty in a variety of ways that are outside formal job postings and best employment practices. Adjunct faculty tell stories of being hired sight unseen, with no credential checks and having received no information regarding work expectations. The processes used to hire and evaluate adjunct faculty will be different from those used for full-time faculty, but putting a process in place and following it will signal to adjunct faculty that they are valued.

Equitable treatment affords adjunct faculty opportunities for advancement in ways that are similar to those enjoyed by full-time faculty. One way to accomplish this is to establish a system of rank for adjunct faculty, along the lines of lecturer, senior lecturer I, and senior lecturer II, based on established criteria for advancement and with an increase in base pay at each step. Although promotions within such a system of adjunct ranks do not offer the same benefits of tenure, they are recognition of the value of the individual and an acknowledgment that experience and continuing growth in the teaching practice should be rewarded. The same equitable treatment should be provided in professional development. As full-time faculty have access to professional development, so should adjunct faculty, including support for academic conference participation and research grants. Although providing such opportunities may not be possible at the same levels for adjunct faculty as for full-time faculty, making such opportunities available signals that the institution values adjunct faculty who are striving to improve their teaching skill set.

Providing full benefits to adjunct faculty undermines the primary motive for adjunct employment in the first place, namely, saving money, but rethinking the benefits issue can improve adjunct faculty's attitudes and reduce feelings of second-class status they commonly feel. Lack of benefits such as health insurance may drive adjunct faculty to seek additional courses at multiple institutions to cover these expenses. Even allowing adjunct faculty the opportunity to buy into group medical plans offered by the institution can be helpful and is little cost to the institution. Concerns about the increased cost of providing benefits to adjunct faculty can be mitigated by limits on benefits based on length of service or minimum course loads. Providing such benefits to continuing adjunct faculty is another way of recognizing the value of their service and promotes healthier attitudes. Most adjunct faculty do not expect the same benefits that full-time faculty receive, but having policies, procedures, and benefits that in some ways parallel those offered to full-time faculty promotes feelings of inclusion and self-worth.

Professional Development

As our interest and experience with delivering adjunct faculty development opportunities was the impetus for this book, it is appropriate that our final section focuses on professional development. In our experience, when adjunct faculty are properly supported in their teaching and have access to professional development opportunities, learning by their students is equivalent to that of students who are taught by full-time instructors. This highlights the need to offer adjunct faculty the same types of opportunities as are usually afforded to full-time faculty. All faculty members need guidance in course design, pedagogy, proper use of technology, best practices in assessment, access to resources, and support services. In other words, they need training and the opportunity to participate in communities where such training is not only offered but also encouraged and where colleagues, be they full-time or part-time, are supportive of an institutional culture that values teaching.

Although the needs of adjunct faculty in regard to professional development are in many ways the same as those for full-time faculty, their diverse situations and part-time status affect how to best support them. Offering development programs and opportunities at times when adjunct faculty can attend runs counter to a culture where such opportunities are scheduled around the needs of full-time faculty and staff. Offering orientations and programs at times conducive to adjunct participation is the solution but one that may require additional, or a reallocation of, resources. Compensating adjunct faculty for participation in professional development also demonstrates that their time is valuable and that the institution values their efforts to improve their teaching.

A vital part of any professional development program is finding ways to acknowledge the participation of adjunct faculty. Certificates, badges, and letters sent to chairs, deans, and other supervisory personnel are all ways to demonstrate gratitude and are tangible ways of acknowledging the contributions of adjunct faculty whose motivations for a teaching career vary but who all appreciate the recognition. Completion of adjunct faculty institutes, teaching academies, or other training programs can also be rewarded by increases in base pay levels, further promoting the value of professional development to the adjunct community and resulting in improved teaching across the institution.

As adjunct faculty continue to grow in both numbers and diversity, their impact on the student experience grows as well. They are no longer "invisible." Adjunct faculty are increasingly the face of the institution, yet their voices remain muted or unheard by administrators. For colleges and universities under increasing pressure to raise graduation rates and demonstrate student success, providing professional development opportunities for all faculty is no longer a luxury they cannot afford. Every institution of higher learning, regardless of size and available resources, can improve the conditions for adjunct faculty by focusing on these four themes: identification, community, equitable treatment, and professional development. Our hope is that the stories we shared will not only increase awareness of the need and benefits of professional development for adjunct faculty but also inspire those in positions of influence to develop and implement programs and strategies in support of this expanding segment of the academic workforce.

Afterword: Continuing the Conversation

Our goal has been to bring adjunct faculty voices out of the shadows and into the national conversation about the current state of teaching employment in American higher education. This conversation not only involves the role and working conditions of adjunct faculty but also has raised larger questions about the impact of current instructor hiring models on quality education for our students. Additional stories from adjunct faculty can be found at https://sty.presswarehouse.com/Books/BookDetail.aspx?productID=463406

References

American Association of University Professors. (2016). *Higher education at a crossroads: The annual report on the economic status of the profession, 2015–16*. Washington, DC: Author. Retrieved from https://www.aaup.org/report/higher-education-crossroads-annual-report-economic-status-profession-2015-16

Coalition on the Academic Workforce. (2012). *A portrait of part-time faculty members: A summary of findings on part-time faculty respondents to the Coalition on the Academic Workforce survey of contingent faculty members and instructors*. Retrieved from http://www.academicworkforce.org/CAW_portrait_2012.pdf

Gappa, J. M., & Leslie, D. W. (1993). *The Invisible Faculty: Improving the Status of Part-Timers in Higher Education*. San Franscisco, CA: Jossey-Bass.

Kezar, A. (2012). Spanning the great divide between tenure-track and non-tenure-track faculty. *Change, 44*(6), 6–13.

Appendix

Exploring the State of Adjunct Faculty Development: A Survey of Faculty Developers

Kimberly Smith, Roy Fuller, and Marie Kendall Brown

Institutional and Faculty Development Structure Information: The following questions seek to determine both the type of institution at which you serve and the overall nature of your faculty development structure.

1. What is your institution's Carnegie classification (2010)?
    a. Associate's Colleges
    b. Doctorate-Granting Universities
    c. Master's Colleges and Universities
    d. Baccalaureate Colleges
    e. Special Focus Institutions
    f. Tribal Colleges
    g. Other (please describe) _____

2. Is your institution:
    a. Public
    b. Private

3. Which best describes your institution's faculty development structure?
    a. A centralized unit with dedicated staff that offers a range of faculty development programs
    b. A "clearinghouse" for programs and offerings
    c. A committee charged with supporting faculty development
    d. An individual faculty member or administrator charged with supporting faculty development
    e. Other (please describe) _____

4. Who is the primary audience for your faculty development programs and services? Please mark all that apply.
   a. Full-time faculty
   b. Part-time faculty
   c. Staff
   d. Graduate students

5. Current practices: Please indicate the extent to which your faculty development program has offered or is currently offering services pertaining to each of the following topics and issues:

   1 = has never offered, 2 = offered in the past, 3 = occasionally offered, 4 = frequently offered

Current Practices	1	2	3	4
Assessment of student learning outcomes				
Teaching underprepared students				
The shifting characteristics/demographics of students				
Integrating technology into "traditional" teaching and learning settings				
Teaching in online and distance environments				
Multiculturalism and diversity related to teaching				
Teaching for student-centered learning				
Teaching nontraditional (adult) learners				
Critical thinking				
Writing across the curriculum/writing to learn				
Team teaching				
Course/teaching portfolios				
Classroom observation				
Peer review				
Course and curriculum reform				
General education reform				
Community service-learning				
Other				

6. If you selected "Other," please describe:
   Response: _____

7. Do adjunct faculty participate in your programs/services?
   a. Yes (*Note:* These respondents continue to next question.)
   b. No (*Note:* These respondents skip ahead to Question 17.)

8. How do adjuncts participate in your faculty development programs?
   a. All our professional development programs are open, and adjuncts are free to participate.
   b. Some of our programs are status-specific, and adjuncts are not our target audience.
   c. We offer specific programs targeting adjunct faculty only.
   d. Other (please describe) _____

9. To the best of your knowledge, what percent of participants in your institution/Center for Teaching and Learning's (CTL) faculty development programs are adjunct faculty?
   a. Less than 10%
   b. 10% to 20%
   c. 21% to 40%
   d. More than 41%

Adjunct Faculty Development Program Goals and Purposes: The following questions are designed to explore adjunct faculty development as offered by your institution and/or CTL.

10. Does your institution/CTL offer professional development opportunities *specifically* designed to meet the needs of adjunct faculty?
    a. Yes
    b. No

11. Which types of programs are offered specifically in support of adjunct faculty? Check all that apply:
    a. Orientation sessions
    b. Faculty Learning Communities
    c. Single sessions on specific teaching and learning topics
    d. Reading groups featuring teaching and learning topics
    e. Certificate programs for adjuncts (single or multiple session)
    f. Classroom observation
    g. Classroom technology training

h. Brown-bag lunch sessions
i. Mentoring opportunities
j. Other (please describe) _____

12. Faculty development may be guided by various goals and purposes. Please indicate the extent to which faculty development at your institution/CTL is guided by any of the following.

1 = not at all, 2 = very little, 3 = somewhat, 4 = to a great extent

Goal or purpose	1	2	3	4
a. To respond to and support individual adjunct faculty members' goals for professional development				
b. To foster collegiality within and among faculty members and/or departments				
c. To create or sustain a culture of teaching excellence				
d. To provide recognition and reward for excellence in teaching				
e. To advance new initiatives in teaching and learning				
f. To act as a change agent within the institution				
g. To respond to critical needs as defined by the institution				
h. To provide support for faculty members who are experiencing difficulties in their teaching				
i. To support departmental goals, planning, and development				
j. To position the institution at the forefront of educational innovation				
k. Other				

13. If you selected "Other," please describe:
Response: _____

14. Using the letters from the list, please indicate the three primary purposes that guide your program, beginning with the most important. Example: a, k, f
Response: _____

15. Program influences: Adjunct faculty development programs may be influenced by a variety of factors. Please indicate the extent to which each factor influences the focus and activities of your adjunct faculty development programs.

    1 = not at all, 2 = very little, 3 = somewhat, 4 = to a great extent

Factor	1	2	3	4
Full-time faculty interests and concerns				
Part-time faculty interests and concerns				
Priorities of department chairs and deans				
Priorities of senior-level institutional leaders				
Priorities of the director or person leading your program				
Immediate organizational issues, concerns, or problems				
Institutional strategic plan				
Your faculty development program's strategic plan				
Priorities indicated in the higher education or faculty development literature				
Other				

16. If you selected "Other," please describe:
    Response: _____

17. Adjunct faculty development programs are sometimes influenced by ideas that have been implemented in other institutions' programs. If other programs in adjunct faculty development have served as models for your efforts or influenced your program, please list the institution(s):
    Response: _____

18. Does your institution/CTL offer incentives to adjunct faculty who use your programs and services?
    a. Yes   (*Note:* These respondents continue to next.)
    b. No   (*Note:* These respondents skip ahead to Question 20.)

19. What incentives do you offer to adjunct faculty who use your programs and services?
    a. Financial incentives paid to faculty

b. Free learning resources (e.g., scholarship of teaching and learning books, access to webinars)
c. Certification for teaching modules/sessions completed
d. Letters of recommendation for chairs, deans, and so on
e. Free parking for programs
f. Other (please describe) _____

Adjunct Empowerment: The following questions address the growing unionization movement among adjunct faculty, as well as the extent to which adjunct faculty have a voice in faculty governance at your institution.

20. Unionization: Does your institution have any of the following?
    a. An existing union for full-time faculty
    b. Union organizing activities
    c. An existing union for part-time faculty
    d. Do not know

21. Does your faculty governance structure allow for the direct participation of adjunct faculty?
    a. Yes
    b. No

22. If yes, please describe: _____

23. Are there adjunct-specific organizations on your campus?
    a. Yes
    b. No

24. If yes, please describe: _____

Open Response: The following questions will help us identify programs and perspectives that can assist us as we document the current status of adjunct faculty development.

25. If you had to identify one thing (program, service, etc.) that your institution/CTL does well in support of adjunct faculty, what would it be?
    Response: _____

26. If you could do one thing (program, service, etc.) to improve professional development for adjunct faculty at your institution, what would it be?
    Response: _____

27. What other information would you like to provide about how your institution/CTL supports adjunct faculty?
Response: _____

28. As a faculty developer, what do you think are the most significant challenges in supporting adjunct faculty and why?
Response: _____

Demographic Data: The following questions will assist us as we develop a profile of adjunct faculty developers.

29. Please indicate which of the following roles apply to you:
    a. Director
    a. Assistant/Associate Director
    b. Program Coordinator
    c. Technology Coordinator
    d. Senior-Level Administrator
    e. Instructional Development Consultant
    f. Faculty Member
    g. Other (please describe) _____

30. If you have multiple roles, please indicate your primary title:
Response: _____

31. Do you have a faculty appointment?
    a. Yes
    b. No

32. If yes, please indicate your discipline/field:
Response: _____

33. What is your current employment status?
    a. Full-time
    b. Part-time

34. How long have you held a position of responsibility in faculty development? Total years (whole number):
Response: _____

Final Question:

35. We welcome any additional comments about these issues or this survey.
     Thank you!
     Response: _____

Editors and Contributors

Editors

Roy Fuller, PhD, is an adjunct professor in comparative humanities at the University of Louisville and adjunct professor of theology at Bellarmine University.

Marie Kendall Brown, PhD, is assistant director for faculty development at the Delphi Center for Teaching and Learning at the University of Louisville.

Kimberly Smith, MS, received her degree in counseling and personnel services with a concentration in college student personnel from the University of Louisville.

Contributors

Anne M. Acker, MA, LPC, is an adjunct professor in psychology and a mental health counselor for students at Saginaw Valley State University.

Lester L. Altevogt, MS, is an adjunct instructor of mathematics at Saginaw Valley State University.

Larry Bonde, MBA, is an adjunct instructor in the Math and Science Department at Kirkwood Community College in Cedar Rapids, Iowa.

Summer Cherland, PhD, is an adjunct faculty member in history, reading, and Chicano studies at GateWay Community College and Estrella Mountain Community College. She currently collaborates in the oversight of the Adjunct Faculty Excellence in Teaching Academy at GateWay Community College.

Ann Coburn-Collins, MA, is an adjunct professor in sociology and gender studies and is the director of academic programs support at Saginaw Valley State University.

Heather Crook, MA, teaches English and composition at Arizona State University and GateWay Community College.

Lindsey Dippold, PhD, is a clinical assistant professor in higher education at Arizona State University, and she currently collaborates in the oversight of the Adjunct Faculty Excellence in Teaching Academy at GateWay Community College.

Ruth Fagan, LCSW, PhD, is an adjunct professor at the University of Texas at Austin, School of Social Work, Austin.

J.W. Gaberdiel, MEd, teaches high school mathematics and science by day and enjoys teaching mathematics as an adjunct instructor at GateWay Community College and Phoenix College in the evenings.

Brandon Hensley, PhD, is a visiting assistant professor and coordinator of assessment in the Department of Communication and Organizational Leadership at Millikin University.

Bridget A. Kriner, MA, is a doctoral student in urban education at Cleveland State University and an adjunct faculty member at Cuyahoga Community College.

Andrea McCourt, PhD, is the program director for the human resource development academic program at Texas Tech University. During her career, McCourt has been an adjunct faculty member at several institutions, including Texas Tech and the University of Maryland University College.

Chris Potts, MA, is a PhD candidate at Claremont Graduate University and a lecturer for the English Department at California State University, Dominguez Hills.

Paul G. Putman, PhD, is a donor relations officer at the Cleveland Foundation and an adjunct instructor in the diversity management graduate program at Cleveland State University.

Jenalee Remy, MC, is an adjunct faculty member in counseling and personal development for GateWay Community College. She teaches college and career success and multiculturalism.

Victoria Shropshire, MA, is a PhD candidate at the University of Glasgow and previously served as an adjunct instructor in English at Elon University.

Suzanne Tapp, MA, is the executive director of the Teaching, Learning, and Professional Development Center and an adjunct faculty member in the Integrated Studies program at Texas Tech University (TTU). Tapp also teaches in the TTU first-year seminar program called Raider Ready and enjoys both face-to-face and online learning experiences.

Lisa S. Tsay, MPhil, is an adjunct instructor of philosophy at Saginaw Valley State University.

Index

new FACULTY MAJORITY